Scholastic Children's Books,
Commonwealth House, 1-19 New Oxford Street,
London WC1A 1NU, UK

A division of Scholastic Ltd
London ~ New York ~ Toronto ~ Sydney ~ Auckland
Mexico City ~ New Delhi ~ Hong Kong

Published in this edition by Scholastic Ltd, 2000
Cover illustration copyright © Tony De Saulles, 2000

Bulging Brains
First published in the UK by Scholastic Ltd, 1999
Text copyright © Nick Arnold, 1999
Illustrations copyright © Tony De Saulles, 1999

Disgusting Digestion
First published in the UK by Scholastic Ltd, 1998
Text copyright © Nick Arnold, 1998
Illustrations copyright © Tony De Saulles, 1998

ISBN 0 439 99749 6

Printed by WS Bookwell, Finland

10 9 8 7 6 5 4 3 2 1

The right of Nick Arnold and Tony De Saulles to be identified as the author and
illustrator of this work respectively has been asserted by them in accordance
with the Copyright, Designs and Patents Act, 1988.

Contents

Bulging Brains

Disguting Digestion

BULGING BRAINS

Nick Arnold has been writing stories and books since he was a youngster, but never dreamt he'd find fame writing about Horrible Science. His research involved battling with threadworms, bathing in stomach acid and volunteering for brain surgery and he enjoyed every minute of it.

Nick's hobbies include eating pizza, riding his bike and thinking up corny jokes (though not all at the same time).

Tony De Saulles picked up his crayons when he was still in nappies and has been doodling ever since. He takes Horrible Science very seriously and even agreed to sample several school dinners and sketch a live brain operation. Fortunately, he has made a full recovery.

When he's not out with his sketchpad, Tony likes to write poetry and play squash, though he hasn't written any poetry about squash yet.

INTRDUCTION

To hear some scientists talk you'd think they knew everything about science...

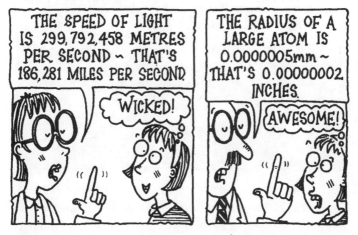

But don't be fooled – scientists *don't* know everything. After all, if they did there would be no need for any new experiments. Scientists could sit around all day with their feet up. But, in fact, there are lots of mysteries left to solve. Lots of things we don't know or don't understand.

For example, there's one object that's so mysterious it makes the brainiest scientists scratch their heads. It's wet and squishy and looks revolting – and oddly enough, it's found between their ears. What is it? No, it's not their disgusting, snotty nose. It's the bit *inside* their heads – their bulging brain. Scientists aren't even sure how it works...

But if scientists are puzzled by their own little grey cells what chance do the rest of us have? No wonder learning about your brain can make your head ache.

THE MEDULLA OBLONGATA IS CONNECTED TO THE PONS... BLAH... DRONE... WITTER

GROAN! ACHE! THROB!

Well, if science scrambles your brains, help is at hand. This book is bulging with brain facts. For example, bet you never knew that in 1998 US scientists found the part of the brain that makes you laugh. They gave an electric shock to this area of a girl's brain and she started giggling uncontrollably.

THIS IS NO LAUGHING MATTER

HA HA! GIGGLE! GIGGLE!

And that's not all. Did you know that in one brain experiment children were forced to sniff their little brother's stinky old T-shirts? (Page 54 will give you all the smelly details.) Now that really is cruelty!

So by the time you've finished reading this book your knowledge will be so vast you could easily become the brains of your class. And who knows? Your teacher might even mistake you for a scientific mega-genius. But to enjoy the full benefits you've got to ask your brain to help you read this book.

Your eyeballs scan the letters, your brain makes sense of the words, and your memory reminds you what they mean. But hold on – looks like you've already started ... oh well, don't let me stop you. Now ask your brain to send a message down thousands of nerves to tell your finger muscles to gently lift the next page.

Dr Funkenstain felt a rush of excitement as she gazed into the glass tank. For five years she had been planning this experiment. Now she had done it and she was looking at the result. The tank was bathed in an eerie light. And floating ghostlike in the tank's centre was a strange and horrible looking object. It was pink like a sausage and wrinkled like an old walnut. And it gave out the faintest whiff of blue cheese.

Could it be an unknown creature from the depths of the ocean? Or perhaps an alien from another world? Dr Funkenstain knew better. She was gazing at a real human brain. A very special human brain because...

IT'S ALIVE!

Dr Funkenstain whispered excitedly. Peering closer she could see the tiny wormlike blood vessels criss-

10

crossing the brain's surface. Dr Funkenstain had done it. She was the first scientist in history to keep a brain alive outside the body.

DON'T PANIC! It's only a story. Scientists can't keep human brains in tanks – yet. But this technique might be possible in the future. Perhaps you'd like to become the first brain surgeon to keep a brain in a tank? If so beware: it's a bad idea to rush into brain surgery without getting to know a bit about your subject. Important facts like...

What's your brain for?

The brain is the part of your body that tells you what's going on around you. You can use your brain to order your body around and even to order everybody else around. But there's much more to your brain. Much, much more.

Inside your brain are your precious memories, your dreams, your hopes for the future and the knowledge of everything you love and care about. In your brain you can sense lovely smells and tastes and colours. Your brain helps you feel great and happy about life and that's the good side. But your brain also creates horrible fears and worries that can make you miserable.

Your brain makes the thoughts and feelings that make your personality. Your brain turns your body from a living object into *you* the person. Without a brain you'd be as dead as a dodo's tombstone, so it's good to know that you've got your very own bulging brain right now between your ears ... hopefully.

Inside the bulging brain

Still want to be a brain surgeon? Excellent. Now you've found out a bit about what the bulging brain does, you're ready to check out how it works...

Bulging fact file

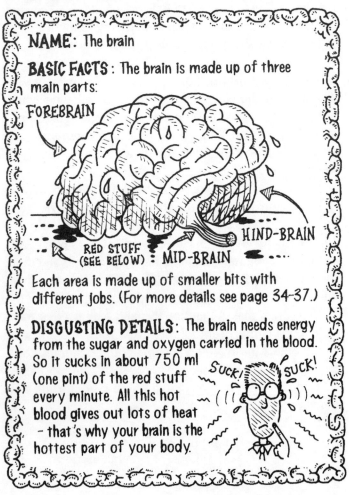

NAME: The brain

BASIC FACTS: The brain is made up of three main parts:

FOREBRAIN

HIND-BRAIN

RED STUFF (SEE BELOW) : MID-BRAIN

Each area is made up of smaller bits with different jobs. (For more details see page 34–37.)

DISGUSTING DETAILS: The brain needs energy from the sugar and oxygen carried in the blood. So it sucks in about 750 ml (one pint) of the red stuff every minute. All this hot blood gives out lots of heat – that's why your brain is the hottest part of your body.

SUCK! SUCK!

Have you got a bulging brain?

So just how clever is your brain? Well, if you're going to be a brain surgeon you'll need to know all the answers to this brain-teasing quiz:

1 What happens if half your brain is damaged?

a) It doesn't half hurt, ha-ha. No, seriously, you can't remember anything.

b) You die. No one could survive such a terrible injury.

c) You can live normally although you have to re-learn vital skills such as talking.

2 What happens if someone cuts your brain in two?

a) Your brain becomes twice as clever.

b) Your brain functions normally but you may find yourself doing your science homework twice.

c) Each side of your brain behaves like a separate person.

3 Imagine you were born without 97 per cent of your cortex (cor-tex) – that's the wrinkly part of your brain at the top where you do your thinking. You're left with a tiny slice of brain in this area. What would happen to you?

a) You'd be left with the brains of a half-witted stick insect.

b) You'd be as brainy as anyone else ... but only for five minutes a day. The rest of the time you'd blunder around like a zombie in a horror movie.

c) Your brain would work normally and you could be as brainy as your science teacher. (Yes, teachers are said to be intelligent.)

4 What would you feel if someone stuck a finger into your brain and waggled it about?

a) Unbearable agony – the worst pain in the world.

b) You'd feel hot and cold shivers all over your body.

c) Nothing because the brain cannot feel touch.

5 How much energy does your brain use in a science test?

a) Such a small amount that it can't be measured (especially if you don't know the answers).

b) Enough to light up the classroom. No wonder the test makes you light-headed, ha-ha.

c) Just enough to power a dim light bulb.

6 Why do you feel tired after the test?

a) All that mental effort strains the brain.

b) During the test your brain drew extra energy in the form of sugar in your blood. After the test your body feels tired because it lacks this vital blood sugar.

c) You were so tense your muscles bunched up and used up energy. And your muscles feel tired – not your brain.

7 How much of your brain is water?

a) About 5 per cent

b) 32 per cent

c) About 80 per cent

Answers:

All the answers are **c)**, so you can check them without taxing your brain too much. And here are a few more details to get you thinking.

1 A bump on the head can injure the brain (see pages 131-141 for the grisly details). Yet the brain can survive dreadful injuries. If one half of the brain is injured, the half that's left learns how to do the work of the damaged half.

2 This operation was performed in the 1960s on patients suffering from violent fits. The operation stopped the fits from spreading through the brain. But afterwards the two sides of the brain acted like separate people. One woman tried to put on a different shirt with each hand. She ended up wearing two shirts.

3 People can be perfectly intelligent with very little cortex. This condition is caused by a disease called hydrocephalus (hi-dro-cef-al-us). This results in too much fluid sloshing around the skull, so there's less room for the brain.

4 Your nerves take signals from elsewhere in your body to your brain. This means you actually experience pain, touch, taste, smell, sound and vision in your brain. But oddly enough, there are no touch sensors on the brain itself. (You'll find the low-down on senses on pages 47-66.)

5 Yes, in light bulb terms we're all rather dim. Scientist Louis Sokoloff of the US National Institute of Mental Health has found the brain uses the same amount of energy gazing dreamily at a sunset as it does in a tough science test. So what would you rather do?

6 If the questions were really easy, and you managed to relax in the science test, you wouldn't feel so whacked.

7 That's why when you become a brain surgeon and get to touch a brain it'll feel like squidgy blancmange or a soft-boiled egg. The brain needs water for vital chemical reactions such as sending nerve signals. Without water, a brain begins to overheat and starts to see things that aren't there. Ultimately it will die.

Bulging brain secrets

Psst – wanna know a brain secret? There's more to your brain than water. For example, your brain's made up of millions of cells and each one is so small you need a microscope to see it. (No, these aren't cells that people get locked up in.) Read on, your brain might learn something...

Bulging brain cells

1 Your brain is bulging with 100,000,000,000 – that's 100 *billion* – nerve cells or neurons. These are special cells used for sending signals inside the brain. If you don't believe it, try counting them yourself.

2 Each cell is a living blob and some are so tiny that you can fit 25 on to this fullstop. (You'll need a steady hand for this.)

3 If you laid the cells from just one brain in a line they would stretch 1000km – a quarter of the way across the USA.

4 Unborn babies grow new brain cells at the rate of 2,000 every *second*. And all your brain cells were already in place when you were born. But after you get to 25, about 12,000 cells die each day (that's 4.4 million a year).

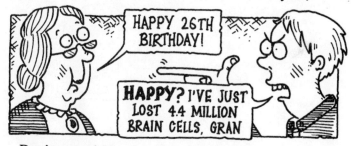

Don't worry! You can lose cells at this rate for a lifetime and still have 98 per cent of them left.

5 Your brain cells are desperate for oxygen. Starve a brain of blood for just seven seconds and it goes on strike and switches itself off. You might call this fainting. Scientists aren't quite sure how this fascinating process takes place.

Yep – even now scientists are baffled by the mysterious brain. But not quite as baffled as the people who first probed the brain's grisly secrets. Check out the next page and prepare to be baffled, bewildered, bemused and ... *horrified*.

BULGING BRAIN BOFFINS

The first brain surgeons had a problem. The bulging brain is mysterious because you get no clues to tell you what's going on inside it. I mean there's no helpful sign saying...

BE QUIET, I'M THINKING

Unlike certain other parts of the body the brain doesn't do interesting things like digest food, burp or even fart. The brain just sits around all day squelching to itself.

CUT HERE

YOU'RE BETTER OFF WITHOUT IT SIRE... ALL THAT SQUELCHING

So it's not so surprising that these early pioneers made some mind-boggling mistakes.

Mind-boggling mistakes

The ancient Egyptians and Greeks thought that the thinking part of the body was the heart. This seemed right because your heart beats faster when you're upset or excited. Is that why your teacher (who could be as old

19

as the pyramids) makes you learn boring facts "by heart"? Well, anyway, the ancient Greeks and Egyptians were *wrong*.

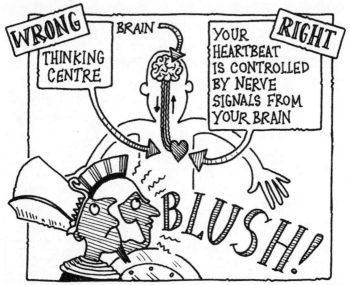

Brainy Greek philosopher Aristotle (384-322 BC) also thought the heart did the thinking. He reckoned the brain was simply a cooling system for the blood. According to Aristotle when you get a cold your cooling system overflows. (That's why snot dribbles out of your nose.)

But he was *wrong* too. Snot is made in the lining of the nose to catch germs and dust. Your nose is runny in a cold because your body is trying to flush out the germs that cause the illness.

Actually, Greek doctor Alcmaeon of Croton (6th century BC) had already figured out what the brain was up to. He cut up dead bodies and noticed that there were nerves running from the eyeballs to the brain. He also noted that patients with head injuries couldn't think clearly. "Clearly," thought Al, "the brain has to be involved in seeing and thinking."

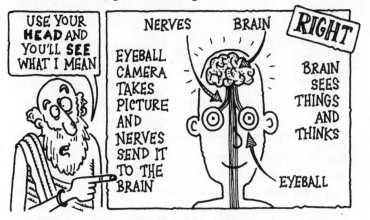

But for over a thousand years doctors remained puzzled. They weren't sure how the brain worked or what the different bits were for. There were theories, of course. One widely held view was that you did your thinking in the fluid-filled spaces inside the brain known as ventricles (ven-trick-als). The rest of the brain was a squelchy bubble- wrap to cushion the vital holes. But by the 18th century scientists were looking at the brain in a more scientific way. And making strange and grisly discoveries...

Bulging brain secrets: Franz Gall (1758-1828)

As a child Franz noticed that one of his school friends had bulging eyes. This boy was good at spelling and Franz wondered if everyone who is good at spelling has bulging eyes. After he became a doctor in Vienna he cut up dead bodies and came to the conclusion that the eyes bulged because the brain behind them was also bulging. Franz reckoned this bulging area dealt with spelling.

Franz was convinced that the size of other brain bulges reflect your personality, for example, whether you're greedy, enjoy smashing things up or have a sense of humour. And to prove this he measured hundreds of skulls of executed criminals and tried to link the bumps he found with the criminals' known personal traits.

Despite his many skulls, er, I mean skills, Franz was on the wrong track. There is no link between the shape of your brain and your personal qualities. But up to the 1850s many people believed Franz had found a way to measure personality. And when Franz's own brain was examined after his death it was found to be smaller than average. Now, I wonder what that could mean?

The talking brain: Paul Broca (1824-1880)

Paul was working as a surgeon in Paris when he met a patient named Tan. "Tan" was his nickname because the poor man had suffered a brain injury that left him unable to speak any word except "tan". Tan was already ill when he saw Broca. Broca could do nothing to help his patient and a few days later he died.

Tan's misfortune was a great opportunity for science. Broca cut open Tan's brain and found that the injury was in what's now imaginatively known as Broca's area (surely it ought to be called Tan's area?). Broca realized that this area of the brain helps you pronounce words properly.

This was a major discovery, but as far as speech goes it wasn't the last word – geddit? In 1874 German scientist **Carl Wernicke (1848-1905)** found another bit (now known – surprise, surprise – as Wernicke's area) which helps you *choose* the right words. People with brain damage in this area often talk utter drivel but with perfect grammar. (For more details see page 77.)

HOW ARE YOU FEELING, TODAY?

LIKE A SHY HADDOCK, MR WERNICKE

The twitching brain: Julius Eduard Hitzig (1838-1907)

If Mrs Hitzig had walked into the bedroom unexpectedly one day in 1870 she would have received a horrible shock. Her husband and his pal Gustav Fritsch were experimenting on a dog's brain using her dressing-table as a workbench.

At the time, Hitzig was working as a doctor in Switzerland but he didn't have a lab of his own. (By the way it's a bad idea to use your mum's dressing-table to practise your brain surgery. You could use the bathroom instead, but make sure you mop the floor afterwards.)

Actually, the dog was getting quite a shock too. An electric shock to the left side of its brain. Hitzig found that this made the dog's right legs twitch. This electrifying test proved that the left side of the brain controls the right side of the body and vice versa. Later in the year war broke out between Germany and France, and Hitzig got the chance to try the same tests on wounded soldiers with bits of their brains shot away. The results confirmed his theory.

As a result of the work of these pioneers, new groups of scientists began to take an interest in the brain. You'll be coming across some of them later on in this book. Here's a handy guide to help you spot them...

Spot the scientist

1. Neurophysiologist
(new-ro-fizzy-olo-gist)

INTERESTED IN: finding out how the brain and nerves work.

WHAT THEY DO: study bits of chopped-up brain and analyse chemicals from the brain.

WHERE THEY WORK: University laboratories or large hospital labs.

2. Neurologists (new-rol-lo-gists)

INTERESTED IN: Studying the brain and nerves, too, but they're especially keen on horrible but fascinating brain and nerve diseases.

WHAT THEY DO: Treat patients with diseases of the nerves and brain. Some of them are also neurosurgeons which is the posh term for brain surgeons.

WHERE THEY WORK: Hospitals.

3. Psychiatrists (si-ki-a-trists)

INTERESTED IN: Diseases of the mind. Psychiatrists are trained as doctors rather than purely scientists.

WHAT THEY DO: Talk to the patient and attempt to find the causes of their illness.

WHERE THEY WORK: general hospitals and psychiatric hospitals and clinics.

4. Psychologists (si-col-lo-gists)

INTERESTED IN:
Studying the brain by looking at the way it makes people behave.

WHAT THEY DO:
Set up experiments to find out how people react in certain situations. Some of these tests are a bit wacky. Some psychologists are interested in diseases of the mind, but unlike psychiatrists they are not trained as doctors.

WHERE THEY WORK: University labs and hospitals.

Peculiar psychologists

The psychologists take their lead from a very peculiar German scientist, and here's his story...

Horrible Science Hall of Fame

Gustav Fechner (1801-1887) Nationality: German
Fechner's brain was always bulging with ideas but his interest in the mind began with a horrible accident. The physics professor was studying light when he blinded himself by looking at the sun. (Something you should never do.) So you could say poor old Gus got blinded by science – geddit. He became so miserable that he went mad for two years.

But one day he was sitting in the garden and he felt a sudden impulse to tear off his bandages. Amazingly, he found he could see again! Incredible colours flooded his brain and he was so excited he imagined he could see brains inside flowers. (Yes, you did read that last bit correctly.) Gus wrote a peculiar book describing how plants have minds. (Believe this and you're a real cabbage-brain.)

Two years later Gus was enjoying a lie-in. Well, maybe "enjoying" is the wrong word. Gus was racking his brains. And not about whether he'd find a toy in his packet of breakfast cereal or how to make contact with a turnip. He was trying to think of a way to study the brain using scientific experiments rather than cutting it open on an operating table. Then he had a brainwave.

All you had to do was measure how the brain reacts to different sensations. For example, in one test Gus shone a light in a volunteer's eyes and slowly increased the brightness until they noticed the change. This allowed him to measure the brain's ability to notice changes in brightness.

Gus had launched a new branch of science called psychology – the study of human behaviour (although the name actually means "study of the mind" in Greek).

And this exciting new science owed its existence to the fact that the scientist fancied an extra snooze. (Tell your parents this story next time you want a lie-in, you never know they might even fall for it.)

Fechner's work was continued by German **Wilhelm Wundt (1832-1920)**, who set up the world's first psychology lab. Wundt never laughed or smiled or joked and spent his entire life working.

SORRY READERS, NO JOKES ALLOWED WITH THIS PICTURE

His books totalled 53,735 pages – that's equal to writing a 500 page book every year for 100 years. He wrote so much that critics complained that it was hard to discover what Wundt actually thought. American psychologist George A. Miller wrote...

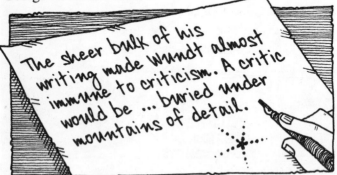

The sheer bulk of his writing made Wundt almost immune to criticism. A critic would be ... buried under mountains of detail.

Brilliant, eh? So if you want to baffle your teacher write a 500 page essay for your science homework. But this tactic didn't stop other psychologists disagreeing with Wundt's approach to psychology. Increasingly they were finding that the brain did a lot more than simply respond to sensations.

Another German psychologist **Max Wertheimer (1880-1943)** wondered if the brain plays tricks to help make sense of a film. A film is made up of thousands of pictures that you see very quickly – about 24 pictures a second. The brain can't keep up with this rapid change so it sees the pictures as a continuously moving scene. So your brain gets the whole picture – and you get the whole movie, including the exciting bits *and* the happy ending.

Max dreamt up this idea on a train in 1910. He was supposed to be on holiday but he excitedly leapt off the train (he waited for it to stop first – he wasn't that excited) and set up experiments to find out why.

Max proved the brain sees the whole scene first and then figures out how the moving objects relate to one another. And he worked out a new theory of psychology called Gestalt (ges-stal-t) based on these ideas. Gestalt actually means "whole" in German and the new theory underlined the importance of finding out how the brain makes sense of things like the film. This was a step forward from Wundt's work, which simply looked at how the brain responds to sensations.

Meanwhile American psychologists such as **John B. Watson (1878-1958)** and, later, **Burrhus Skinner (1904-1990)** were changing the behaviour of rats by training their brains. (You can read more about Watson and his wacky experiments on pages 88-91.)

Bulging brain expressions
Two brain surgeons are quarrelling...

YOU DON'T KNOW AN ALMOND FROM A FRUIT STONE!

Is the quarrel about gardening?

Answer: No. The amygdala (a-mig-dal-a) and putumen (putt-you-men) – almond and fruit stone in Greek – are odd names for areas of the brain.

Confused yet? Well, there are lots more bits and pieces you'll need to know about if you're going to be a brain

30

surgeon. Maybe things would be clearer if you could get your hands on a real dripping brain. Fancy a squidge? Hope so, if not the next chapter's so nasty, it could drive you out of your mind.

Better sharpen that scalpel...

BULGING BRAIN BITS 'n' PIECES

As a brain surgeon you need to know all about the main bits and pieces in the brain. Fortunately we've got hold of a real genuine brain from a real genuinely dead person to help you. Go on, take a peek – it won't bite you.

Brain bits and pieces

The main area you can see is the cortex (that's the wrinkly, thinking bit, remember?).

Dare you discover ... why the cortex is wrinkly?

Ever wondered why brains are wrinkly? Now's your chance to discover the *real* answer...

All you need is:
Two sheets of A4 paper. (Your school report might come in handy here.)

All you do is:
1 Screw one sheet of paper into a tight little ball.

2 Open it up but don't flatten it.
3 Place it over the second sheet of A4 paper.

What do you notice?
a) The screwed-up paper seems to have shrunk.
b) The screwed-up paper has got bigger.
c) Both sheets of paper are the same size.

Answer:
a) The wrinkles and bumps on the paper make it take up less space. The wrinkles on your cortex allow a larger area to squash between your ears. And that's very important because the cortex is very thin – no more than 3 mm (0.12 inches) thick. If your brain was flat it would be the size of a pillowcase and you'd need a huge head to contain it.

To find out more about some of the vital brain bits and pieces let's have a peek at this gory but fascinating medical textbook.

33

BRAIN SURGERY FOR BEGINNERS

Chapter 1: Brain bits and pieces

Cerebrum (ser-ree-brum)

This is the largest bit of the brain – it's so big it makes up 85 per cent of the brain. This area is REALLY important because its wrinkly surface is the cortex, where thinking takes place. The cerebrum is divided into two halves (no one knows the reason for the split). The halves are linked by a bridge at the base made of millions of nerves cells.

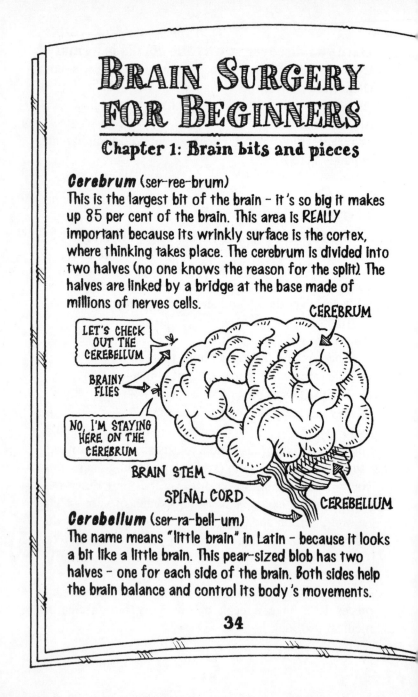

LET'S CHECK OUT THE CEREBELLUM

BRAINY FLIES

NO, I'M STAYING HERE ON THE CEREBRUM

CEREBRUM

BRAIN STEM

SPINAL CORD

CEREBELLUM

Cerebellum (ser-ra-bell-um)

The name means "little brain" in Latin – because it looks a bit like a little brain. This pear-sized blob has two halves – one for each side of the brain. Both sides help the brain balance and control its body's movements.

When you learn a skill such as riding a bike you think about what you're doing. Well, hopefully – otherwise you'd fall off. But after a while you happily pedal around without thinking. Oh, so you knew that? Well, when you stop thinking about what you're doing your cerebellum takes over from your thinking cortex and tells your body what to do. Scientists have found that with the cerebellum in charge you can move faster and less clumsily. (For more details on what the cerebellum can do check out pages 76 and 102.)

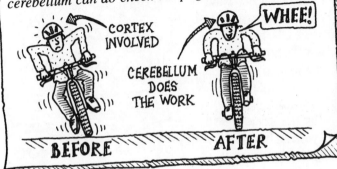

Spinal cord

This is a bundle of nerves 45 cm (18 inches) long and as thick as a thumb. Although it's not technically part of the brain, as a brain surgeon you need to know what it does. It actually takes signals to and from the brain.

Brain stem

This bit links the brain with the spinal cord. It's useful for helping the brain to go to sleep. And it's also useful for waking up the brain to danger or something interesting.

As a brain surgeon you'll need to know a bit more about the even smaller but still vital bits and pieces that lurk deep within the brain. We've cut some brains in half to help you...

Thalamus (thal-a-mus)
You've got two of these – one on either side of the brain. Each thalamus is full of nerve cells, and nerve signals reaching this area can be rerouted to other parts of the brain. What's more, each thalamus passes on messages about smell (that's sniffing whiffs not making them), and the control of some muscles. The thalamus is also involved in helping you remember things.

PINEAL GLAND   HYPOTHALAMUS

PITUITARY GLAND

half a brain (side view)

Hypothalamus (hi-po-thal-a-mus)
A bossy little blob the size of one of your knuckles. It reckons *it's* the boss of the entire body. Controls the water content in the blood, its temperature, sweating, shivering, growing, when you sleep, etc.

The pituitary gland
Vital sidekick for the hypothalamus. Follows its orders and makes the chemicals that go round in the blood. These chemicals, or hormones as scientists call them, order the body to do what the hypothalamus wants.

36

The pineal (pi-nee-al) gland
The name means "pine cone" because it looks a bit like a tiny one. It's sensitive to the amount of light in the day – and this may make you feel tired in the evening and wake you up in the morning. There's a type of fish called a lamprey that has a pineal like an extra eye on top of its head. The extra eye gives it all-round vision. (Scientists have failed to prove the common belief that teachers have this eye in the back of their heads.)

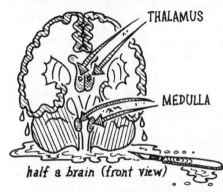

half a brain (front view)

Medulla
Looks after the digestive and breathing jobs. It does this work automatically – which is kind of handy. Just imagine if you had to think how to do these things. You might end up breathing in your supper and then you'd be choking on your food and making a mess on the table.

Limbic (lim-bick) system
An odd mixture of bits and pieces including the amygdala (known in English as the "almond") deep in the brain. Shapes your feelings and is also involved in memory.

WHOOPS! ER, FANCY AN ALMOND SLICE, NURSE?

BRAIN SURGERY FOR BEGINNERS
Chapter 2: Vital brain tests

Of course, as a brain surgeon you'll be performing operations on living patients (hopefully they'll still be alive after the operation too).

DON'T WORRY, I'VE READ A BOOK ABOUT IT!

To help you plan your operations there is an amazing collection of machines that can show what's going on inside the brain before you get cutting. This is useful because you can find out which areas may be damaged or not functioning properly. Let's check them out ...

COMPUTER

X-RAY VIEW INSIDE CAT MACHINE

Machine 1: a CAT
No, this is nothing to do with Tiddles, your pet cat. This CAT is a machine. CAT stands for Computerized Axial Tomography (ax-e-al toe-mog-graf-ee). As a brain expert you should be able to spout this kind of jargon effortlessly. The machine sends weak X-rays through the brain and shows up the result on a computer screen.

Machine 2: a PET

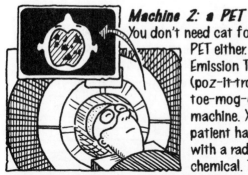

You don't need cat food for this PET either. It's a Positron Emission Tomography (poz-it-tron e-miss-e-on toe-mog-graf-ee) machine. Your poor old patient has to be injected with a radioactive chemical. The scanner detects what happens when the blood takes the chemical into their brain. The blood flows to the bits of the brain that are most active. So you can see what's going on and spot any areas that don't seem to be working properly.

Machine 3: an NMR

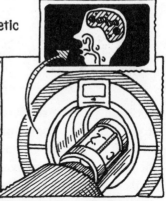

This stands for Nuclear Magnetic Resonance. This nifty device surrounds the brain with a magnetic force and bombards the blood in the brain with radio waves. The atoms (tiny bits that make up chemicals) in the blood bounce back a special type of radio wave that can be detected by the machine. The NMR scan can also show where the blood is flowing inside the brain. More blood flows to the bits of the brain that are thinking, and this can be useful for discovering which areas of the brain are used for particular jobs such as solving maths problems or talking.

39

Machine 4: an EEG

This stands for electroencephalograph (el-leck-tro-en-cef-falo-graf) machine. The metal electrodes pick up electrical signals given off as the brain thinks and the machine displays them as a print-out showing the signals as peaks.

Important note to the reader:

Sorry to interrupt the book. Just a quick message to say that the EEG machine is an ultra-sensitive piece of equipment. This was tested by an American doctor in the mid-1970s who wired up a lime-flavoured jelly to an EEG machine. (The flavour didn't actually affect the test.) According to the machine, the jelly was alive and thinking! In fact, it was reacting to people chatting in the next room. So make sure you read this book q-u-i-e-t-l-y.

Checking the print out
Here's what your EEG print out might show.

1 An alpha rhythm.
This means the
brain's thinking in a
dreamy kind of way.

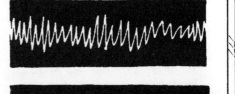

2 Beta rhythm (a
bit faster). The brain
is paying attention
to what's going on.

3 Theta rhythm
(a bit slower). The
brain is feeling
sleepy.

4 Delta rhythm
(very slow). The
brain has fallen into
a deep sleep. (This
has been found to be
a common condition amongst children in science
lessons.)

If the line is completely flat you
should check that your patient
is still alive. A flat line normally
means the patient is dead!

The EEG was invented by German Dr Hans Berger (1873-1941) who spent five years sticking electrodes on people's heads to measure brain activity. He even tested his invention on his children. Hans reckoned he would be able to show what his children and the other patients were thinking. He couldn't do this but he spent another five years writing up his experiments. And then ... no one took any notice.

It wasn't until British Scientist Edgar Adrian (1889-1977) showed that unusual wave patterns could be a sign of brain disease that EEG machines were used in hospitals.

BRAIN SURGERY FOR BEGINNERS

Chapter 3: Surgical tools

Congratulations, you're now almost ready for your first brain operation! First, though, you need to get familiar with a few brain surgeon's tools.

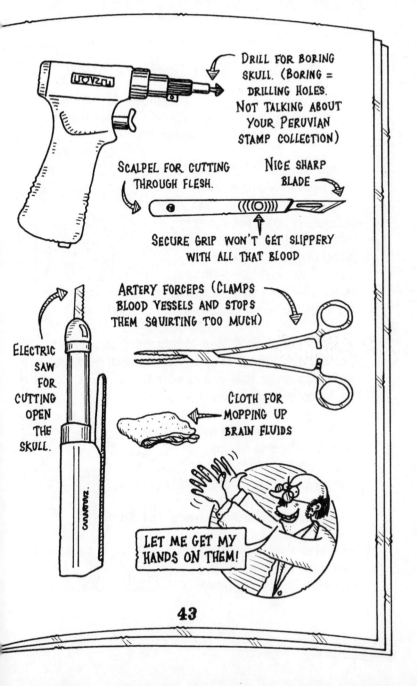

43

Chapter 4: Your first operation

Just before you move on to the surgery bit, take a look at these handy instructions. Better still, keep them by your side during the actual operation.

Brain surgery instructions

1 It helps if you have a particular operation in mind before you begin. For example you might want to remove a blood clot or a fragment of bone after an accident. No responsible brain surgeon would cut open someone's brain just to take a peek inside.

2 Use a PET or NMR scan to help you plan where to cut. In 1998, scientists at Toronto Hospital developed an NMR scanner that you can use to guide your scalpel whilst actually operating.

3 Make sure there are no germs in the area of your operation. It's not enough to clear away the tea things and put the cat out. The entire area should be scrubbed with strong disinfectant to kill germs. You should be thoroughly washed and wear a face mask and a specially disinfected gown.

4 Draw a line on the patient's head to show where you intend to cut. Oops! Nearly forgot. The patient's head should be shaven to prevent bits of hair getting mixed in with their brain.

5 To get at the brain you need to remove a bit of skull. First drill some holes in the skull. (You'll have to concentrate. One slip and you might drill through the brain.)

6 Next, saw between the holes and lift up a flap of skull and meninges (men-in-gees) – the protective layers under the skull. As you lift the meninges you may hear a *sclurping* noise as the clear fluid that surrounds the brain bubbles out.

7 If everything goes according to plan the brain should be pulsing as the blood squirts through its blood vessels.

8 Now to begin your brilliant brain operation...

☠ **HORRIBLE HEALTH WARNING!**

Stop! Don't do anything until you've read the next page!

IMPORTANT AND VERY URGENT ANNOUNCEMENT:

In order to do brain surgery properly you have to study in medical school for at least seven years. You didn't really think you'd be allowed to do brain surgery at your age did you? Sorry to disappoint you. You'd better stick everything back together and be grateful. Why? Because practising brain surgery without proper training could land you in serious legal trouble and result in your pocket money being stopped for 33,000,000 years. Sorry!

Still, there's lots more fascinating things to find out about the brain. For example, there are the amazing ways in which it manages to find out what's going on around you. These are called "senses". So here's a challenge for your brain – has it got the sense to read the next chapter? Better find out!

⚡STARTLING 👁 SENSES⚡

Without senses life would be like sitting in a dark cupboard. Yep, even more boring than a science lesson. But thanks to your brain you are bombarded with startling sights and sounds and smells. It's lucky you've got strong nerves to cope with it all. After all, your senses won't work without nerves...

Bulging fact file

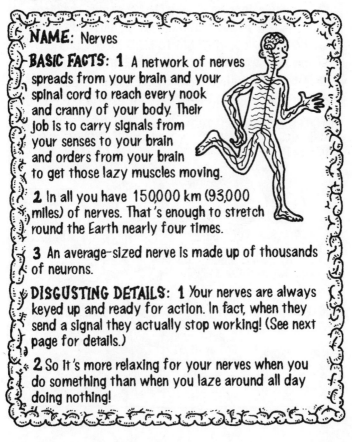

NAME: Nerves

BASIC FACTS: 1 A network of nerves spreads from your brain and your spinal cord to reach every nook and cranny of your body. Their job is to carry signals from your senses to your brain and orders from your brain to get those lazy muscles moving.

2 In all you have 150,000 km (93,000 miles) of nerves. That's enough to stretch round the Earth nearly four times.

3 An average-sized nerve is made up of thousands of neurons.

DISGUSTING DETAILS: 1 Your nerves are always keyed up and ready for action. In fact, when they send a signal they actually stop working! (See next page for details.)

2 So it's more relaxing for your nerves when you do something than when you laze around all day doing nothing!

Your nerves are a bit like an amazing telephone system that takes messages all around your body. Just imagine they were a phone system – the manual would make fascinating reading...

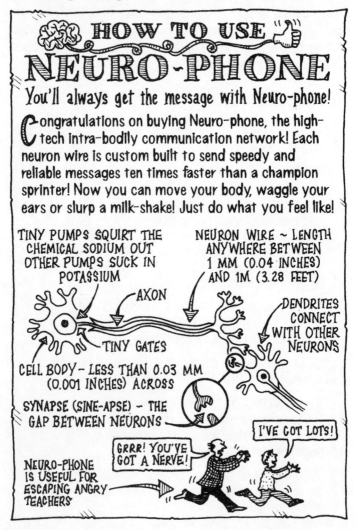

To activate your Neuro-phone system you don't need to worry about boring dialling codes or numbers. Simply ask your brain cortex to send a message anywhere you want in the body. Neuro-phone will do the rest for you. . . here's how.

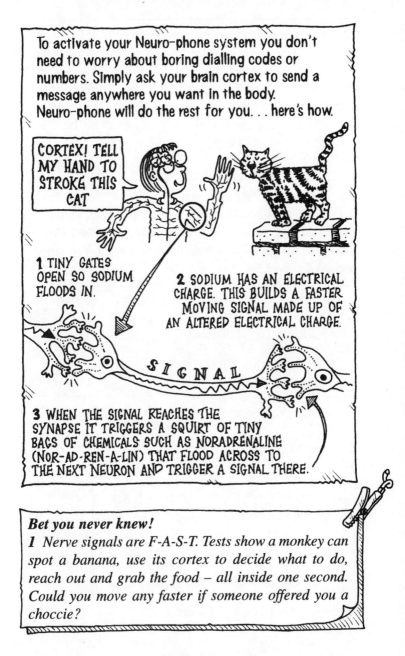

CORTEX! TELL MY HAND TO STROKE THIS CAT

1 TINY GATES OPEN SO SODIUM FLOODS IN.

2 SODIUM HAS AN ELECTRICAL CHARGE. THIS BUILDS A FASTER MOVING SIGNAL MADE UP OF AN ALTERED ELECTRICAL CHARGE.

SIGNAL

3 WHEN THE SIGNAL REACHES THE SYNAPSE IT TRIGGERS A SQUIRT OF TINY BAGS OF CHEMICALS SUCH AS NORADRENALINE (NOR-AD-REN-A-LIN) THAT FLOOD ACROSS TO THE NEXT NEURON AND TRIGGER A SIGNAL THERE.

Bet you never knew!
1 Nerve signals are F-A-S-T. Tests show a monkey can spot a banana, use its cortex to decide what to do, reach out and grab the food – all inside one second. Could you move any faster if someone offered you a choccie?

2 Remember that a science test only produces enough electrical activity in your brain to light a dim light bulb? (See page 15 if you don't.) Well, what do you have to do to light up a Christmas tree? The answer is, even when you're doing nothing there's enough electrical nerve energy in your nervous little body for the job. After all there are no fewer than 100 billion neurons in your body.

Sensational senses

Thanks to your sensational senses you can appreciate the true beauty of the world. A lovely blue cloudless sky, the delicious aroma of new-baked pizza and the soft smooth touch of velvet...

AND ALL THE HORRIBLE BITS TOO, LIKE THE BILE GREEN OF SCHOOL SOUP AND THE STINK OF BAD BREATH AND ITCHY NITS IN YOUR HAIR

YEAH!

Let's take a closer look at these marvellous abilities...

Bulging brain expressions

Some psychologists are chatting over dinner...

MY ANOSMIA IS REALLY BAD

YOU'RE LUCKY IT ISN'T PAROSMIA

Are these weird types of food?

Answer: No. These are problems caused by blows on the head.

Anosmia = you can't smell anything.

Parosmia = all food tastes disgusting. Of course the scientists might have been eating a school dinner. Then their food would have tasted *really* horrible!

Bet you never knew!
The sense of taste gets weaker as we grow older. At present scientists don't understand why this happens, but you can observe the effects any lunchtime. Many children can't stand the vile flavour of school dinners but elderly teachers happily relish the revolting recipes.

Dare you discover ... a touch of the ridiculous?

All you need is:

Your body

Clothes (don't forget to put some on your body)

All you do is:

1 Nothing. If only all science experiments were this easy!

2 Concentrate on trying to feel the clothes you are wearing against your skin. (Don't touch them with your hands.)

What do you notice?

a) I can't feel anything except my itchy socks.

b) I can feel the material against my skin. Funny I never noticed it before.

c) This experiment has given me a headache.

Answer: b) If your nerves feel a constant sensation like your clothes they get used to it and stop firing. That's why you don't feel your clothes and you may forget you're wearing any. Hopefully, you should notice if you're not wearing any.

If **c)** stop concentrating so hard and if **a)** consider the possibility that you're only wearing your socks. This could be a sight for sore eyes, and talking about vision...

Seeing is believing

You might think that you see with your eyes. But your eyeballs simply act like cameras and pick up light patterns from the outside world. It's the brain that makes sense of this information. Sounds complicated? Well, fortunately, the Neuro-phone people have logged the neuron calls involved so you can make sense of it all.

Take a look at this...

You see through your eyeballs. An image of the scene falls on the retina and the one million neurons in your optic nerve take the image in the form of nerve pulses to your brain. Now read on...

1 Retina to thalamus, "GET A LOOK AT THIS!"

RETINA

THALAMUS

2 Thalamus to vision centre at back of cortex, "SOMETHING'S UP. WANNA TAKE A PEEK?"

CORTEX VISION CENTRE

EYEBALL LENS

CHOCCIES

3 Cortex to eyeball muscles, "MOVE THAT EYEBALL ROUND. I WANNA BETTER LOOK"

4 Cortex to eyeball lens muscles, "CAN YOU FOCUS A TEENY BIT MORE?"

5 Meanwhile in the vision centre of the cortex the neurons are chatting away and making sense of what you see...

EYEBALL MUSCLES

LENS MUSCLES

"HEY, SHAPE DEPARTMENT – CAN YOU CHECK OUT THAT SHAPE?"
"LOOKS LIKE A BOX OF CHOCCIES TO ME."

"COLOUR DEPARTMENT – ANY NEWS?"
"IT'S DEFINITELY PINK."

"MOVEMENT DEPARTMENT – ANY ACTION?"
"NOPE – IT'S JUST SITTING THERE."

A message to the reader:
Yep, this is really true. Everything you look at, including this page and these words, is seen *inside* your brain. You also need your brain to make sense of the words (see page 83 for details).

Bet you never knew!
Imagine you're in a science test. At times like this you're concentrating so hard your brain blots out your vision from the corner of your eyes. You also stop hearing background noises because your brain blots these out so you can concentrate on the job you are doing. Scientists aren't sure how your brain performs this useful trick. But without it you'd fail the test and there'd be a terrible BLOT on your school record.

Could you be a scientist?

Scientists at Vanderbilt University, USA, tested some children. The children were blindfolded and given a heap of smelly old T-shirts to sniff. They were asked to spot the distinctive pong of T-shirts belonging to their brothers or sisters. How do you think they got on?

a) The experiment had to be stopped after the horrible stink made some of the children throw up.

b) The children could easily recognize the pong made by their brothers and sisters. They got over 75 per cent of the tests right.

c) The children found it impossible to identify the smell made by their brothers and sisters.

Answer: b) And in tests 16 out of 18 parents could identify their children by their smell. Your sense of smell is better than you may imagine. If you lie on the floor you can actually detect the cheesy pong where someone in a dirty sock walked on the floorboards.

(No need to test this remarkable skill just now.) And you can identify over 10,000 different whiffs and stinks. (Heaven nose how you do it.)

Bringing it all together

Of course in everyday life your brain uses all your senses together to build up a picture of what's going on outside your head. Maybe you'd like to discover how it all slots together. Your mission, should you choose to accept it is to ... (BIG ROLL OF DRUMS HERE) ... eat a chocolate.

(Yep, but it's not as simple it sounds.) Before we start let's listen into those Neuro-phone messages and get an idea of what's involved.

Just a bite

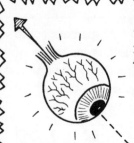

Retina to vision centre and brain stem, "I CAN'T TAKE MY EYES OFF THOSE CHOCOLATES."

Brain stem to cortex, "THERE'S SOMETHING INTERESTING AHEAD. WANNA CHECK IT OUT?"

Cortex to fingers and arms, "EXTEND FINGERS AND PICK UP A CHOCOLATE. HOW DOES IT FEEL?"

Finger-touch receptors to thalamus, "TELL THE CORTEX IT'S LOVELY AND COOL AND SMOOTH AND VELVETY."

Thalamus to sensory area of cortex, "YOU GOT ALL THAT?"

Ears to medulla, "HEY, LISTEN TO THAT LOVELY RUSTLE IN THE BOX."

Medulla to thalamus, "PSST! TELL THE CORTEX TO GET A LOAD OF THIS."

Nose to thalamus, "WOW! WHAT A LOVELY CHOCOLATEY WHIFF – TELL THE CORTEX TO GET A SNIFF OF THIS."

Tongue to cortex, "I'M READY TO SWALLOW. THERE'S LOADS OF SPIT DOWN HERE!"

A note to the reader:
Drooling spit at the sight of a choccie is a reflex (see page 62), triggered by nerves leading from the brain to your gooey saliva glands. Are you starting to drool too? If so, try not to dribble on the nice clean page.

Another note to the reader:
So do you fancy trying this mission for yourself? Chances are you've already had quite a bit of practice.

But if you feel like checking whether your brain can handle all these senses it's worth asking your parents for chocolates. You could explain that you need an extra large box in order to get this vital science experiment absolutely right. And if your parents fall for that, you might as well ask for a day out at a theme park, too.

So how did you get on...?
a) I ate the chocolate so fast I didn't have a chance to follow the instructions.
b) I got muddled up with the instructions and bit my tongue by mistake. Ouch!
c) It was great and all my senses and brain bits worked perfectly.
(If you ticked **a**): oh dear, that's tough, better practise on another choccie. If **b**): you might as well go on to the next section. Because it's a bit of a PAIN too.)

Putting up with pain
Pain is the worst thing you can sense. But you know all about pain already...

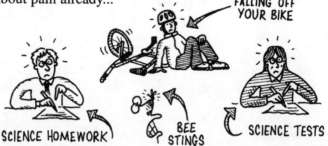

FALLING OFF YOUR BIKE

SCIENCE HOMEWORK

BEE STINGS

SCIENCE TESTS

Dare you discover ... how to put up with pain?
Note to the reader:
This experiment has been banned on the grounds that it's far too cruel. Here are a few facts instead.

A few painful facts

1 Pain is a big trick played by your bulging brain on the rest of your body. Imagine you stub your toe on a stone or even the cat.

You might think you feel the resulting pain in your big toe. But you actually experience the pain in your brain because that's where the nerve signal goes.

2 Your body is crowded with countless thousands of pain receptors. Obviously any damage to the body is red-hot urgent news for the brain – there may be more damage just about to occur so the pain receptors try to let the brain know what's going on NOW.

3 The crushed pain receptors let in a chemical released from the injured areas. This kick starts a nerve signal that blasts up to your brain.

4 The deeper the pain receptors the less sensitive they are – that's why a really bad injury can hurt less than a little scratch. Pain deep in the body often feels like a dull miserable ache.

5 Different pain signals move at different speeds. A sharp prick on your skin hits your brain at 29.9 metres (98 feet) a second. A longer pulse like a burning or aching pain moves through the neurons at a slightly more leisurely 1.98 metres (6.5 feet) a second.

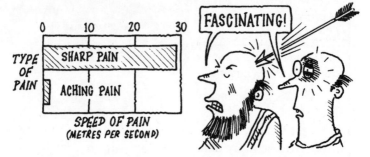

But there's much more to pain than just a horrible feeling in the brain. Here, for a change, is a bit of good news...

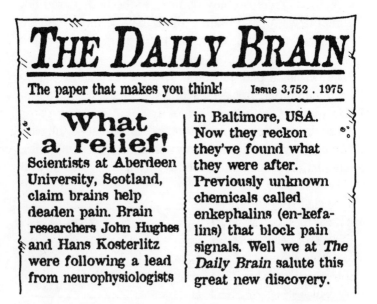

THE DAILY BRAIN

The paper that makes you think!   Issue 3,752 . 1975

What a relief!

Scientists at Aberdeen University, Scotland, claim brains help deaden pain. Brain researchers John Hughes and Hans Kosterlitz were following a lead from neurophysiologists in Baltimore, USA. Now they reckon they've found what they were after. Previously unknown chemicals called enkephalins (en-kefa-lins) that block pain signals. Well we at *The Daily Brain* salute this great new discovery.

If we didn't have these chemicals we're sure they'd be *sorely* missed.

Daily Brain Science Correspondent Dr Alan de Mind writes..

The newly discovered chemicals may explain why taking exercise or other distractions such as a white knuckle ride or an exciting film takes your mind off pain. Presumably doing these things can trigger the brain to make the painkilling chemicals.

Extreme pain

Extremely exciting film

SUPPORTING WEIGHT OF ELEPHANT WITHOUT ENKEPHALINS

SUPPORTING WEIGHT OF ELEPHANT WITH ENKEPHALINS

Bet you never knew!
Another way to deaden pain is to confuse your nerves by getting them to send other signals. So if you bang your shin you could try rubbing it with your hand or a lump of ice. This gets the nerves sending more signals that swamp the pain signals.

The painful truth

Afterwards it's hard to remember exactly what pain is like. Your cruel heartless brain wants every pain you feel to seem really awful and unexpected. That way you'll do something about it. The painful truth is that pain is there so your brain can teach you a painful lesson.

You might think it would be lovely to live in a world without pain. Life would be brilliant, wouldn't it? You could wander around endlessly bumping into things, and not worrying about how much it was going to hurt. Until one day you noticed that your fingers had dropped off. Of course, if you'd felt pain in the first place you'd have got away with a nasty cut rather than no fingers on one hand. By the way, if the thought of all that blood makes you feel like throwing up at this point feel free – being sick, or vomiting to use the technical term, is just another of your...

Action-packed reflexes

Do you do things without thinking? If your answer is "yeah, all the time" then you've probably been making a few reflex actions. Reflexes are actions that your body does in response to startling signals from your senses. These are things like sneezing and coughing and dribbling that you can't stop once they start. (For this reason farting or burping are not reflexes and you've got no excuse for doing them during mealtimes.)

A few more facts you ought to know about reflexes
1 Your brain isn't involved in reflexes. The signals go to

your spinal cord and out again in nerves that control your muscles. This saves time and means that you can whip your hand away from the hot plate of the cooker in 0.03 seconds instead of up to 0.8 seconds if your brain was consulted.

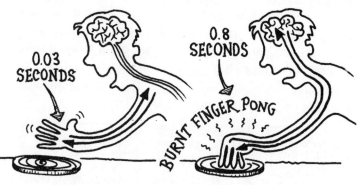

2 Some of the most important work about reflexes was carried out by Russian Ivan Pavlov (1849-1936). Pavlov was a cold unfriendly man who flew into terrible rages if anyone dared criticize him. And no, he wasn't a teacher, he was a scientist.

3 His most famous experiment was to show that you could train dogs to make reflex actions. Dogs dribble when they see food. Pavlov rang a bell every time the dogs were fed. After a while he stopped feeding the dogs but they still dribbled when he rang the bell.

4 Pavlov was so keen on scientific accuracy that he even measured the amount of spit the dogs dribbled. This added no particular value to his work but it showed how seriously he took his job. Would you want a job measuring dog's dribble? If you think it's a mouth-watering opportunity you're a born scientist.

Dare you discover ... a reflex action?

All you need is:
One dog (count first to make sure it's got four legs)

All you do is:
1 Rub the dog's back until the dog reacts.
2 Note what happens next.

What happens next?
a) The dog falls over.

b) The dog scratches its back with its hind legs. (It probably thinks your hand is an extra large flea.)

c) The dog wags its tail and sticks its tongue out and dribbles everywhere.

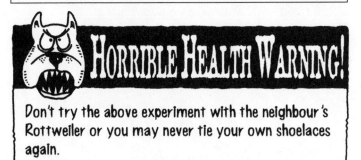

HORRIBLE HEALTH WARNING!

Don't try the above experiment with the neighbour's Rottweiler or you may never tie your own shoelaces again.

65

CONGRATULATIONS! You've successfully read this chapter. Now for the bad news. So far you've been looking at the easy-peasy stuff your brain gets up to. You might find the next chapter rather more mind-bending.

Yep – it's time to put your bulging brain to work.

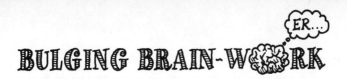

BULGING BRAIN-W🧠RK

Sometimes you need your bulging brain for something more intelligent than scoffing a choccie. Jobs like listening to music, and thinking and talking and reading. Oh, so you don't think they sound too difficult? Well, they are. But don't worry, by the time you've read this chapter you'll have boosted your bulging brainpower. Well, maybe – just a bit.

First sort your left from your right

Your cortex (that's the wrinkly, thinking bit of the brain, remember) is split into two halves. To understand how you use your brain you first need to know how the two halves work together. Bear in mind that one side of the cortex is stronger than the other and takes over most of the work. But which side is that? Well, the diagram below will help you sort that out. But don't forget that the left side of the cortex looks after the right side of the body and vice versa. Got all that?

Anyway, here's the diagram...

X-RAY OF SCIENCE TEACHER'S HEAD

LEFT SIDE OF BRAIN IS IN CONTROL

PEN IN RIGHT HAND

(If the teacher was left-handed these arrangements would be reversed.)

Are you ambidextrous?

Ambidextrous means that you're able to write or draw or hold a tennis racquet or play the guitar or pluck a chicken equally well with both hands.

PLAYING, ER, I MEAN PLUCKING A CHICKEN RIGHT-HANDED AND PLUCKING, OR RATHER PLAYING A GUITAR LEFT-HANDED

This is because neither side of the cortex is stronger than the other. Famous ambidextrous people include English artist Sir Edwin Landseer (1802-1873) who often drew a horse with his right hand and a stag with his left hand at the same time. Try it for yourself – it's much harder than it sounds.

Test your teacher

Is your teacher left-handed, right-handed or ambidextrous? Well, this teacher teasing test will certainly keep her brain fully occupied until the end of the class. By the way, if you're feeling kind you can give your teacher one clue before you start the test: all the answers are for right-handed people.

1 Are babies always...

a) Left-handed?

b) Right-handed?

c) Ambidextrous?

2 Which side of your brain do you use for working out hard maths questions?

a) The left.
b) The right.
c) Neither, I use a calculator.

3 Which side of your brain do you use for having a chat with your friends?
a) The left.
b) The right.
c) The left for chatting with friends but the right when talking to important people like the Head Teacher.

IT'S NOT GOOD ENOUGH, SMITH – I EXPECT YOU TO USE BOTH SIDES WHEN TALKING TO ME

4 Which part of your brain do you use for painting a watercolour?
a) The left.
b) The right.
c) Neither, it's the cerebellum that does the work.

I USE THE WHOLE BRAIN – IT MAKES NICE PATTERNS

5 How do Japanese people differ from the usual right–left division of work within the brain?
a) They use both sides of their brains for talking.
b) Annoying insect sounds trigger brain activity on the left side of their brains instead of the right for everyone else.
c) They can talk aloud without their brains showing unusual activity.

1 c) In babies, both halves of the cortex are equally strong. One side doesn't take over until the child is about two.

2 a) If you're right-handed you read, write and work out sums mostly using the left part of your brain. (If you're left-handed you are more likely to use the right side of your brain for these tasks.)

3 a) The left side also deals with talking aloud. The poor old right side has to spend its life listening to the left side nattering.

4 b) At least the right side of the brain gets to deal with all the enjoyable artistic jobs like making a collage or drawing.

5 b) This finding was reported by Japanese scientist Tsunoda Tadanobu. Some Japanese words sound like insect or water sounds. So the scientist suggested Japanese people listen to these sounds with the left side of their brains that normally deals with language. (Award your teacher an extra mark if they managed to explain this theory.)

Bet you never knew!

For reasons that scientists don't quite understand...
You see things at the back of your cortex (not at the front, which is where your eyes are). You see things to the left in the right side of your brain.
Things to the right get seen in the left side.

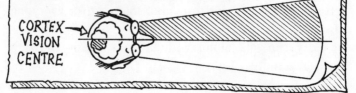

CORTEX
VISION
CENTRE

Dare you discover ... if you're left- or right-eyed?

Your left eye is controlled by the right side of your brain and vice-versa. But which side of your brain is stronger? Here's how to find out...

All you need is:
A finger (preferably one of your own)
Two eyes (these should definitely be your own)
A stationary object 1 metre away (it doesn't matter what this object is. It could be a picture, the wallpaper or even a dead wombat)
A ruler

All you do is:
1 Stick your finger 12 cm (5 inches) in front of your nose.
2 Focus your eyes on the stationary object. The finger should appear out of focus. Note the position of the finger.
3 Now wink each of your eyes in turn.

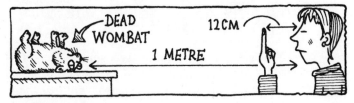

What do you notice?
a) Nothing and people started asking me whom I was winking at. It was all very embarrassing.
b) Each time I winked an eye the finger seemed to jump sideways.
c) The finger seemed to stay where it was when I winked one eye and jump sideways when I winked the other.

Could you be a scientist?

When you listen to music the following areas of your brain are involved...

In the 1970s US neurophysiologists Joseph Bogen and Harold Gordon studied these areas. They injected a powerful painkiller into blood vessels that fed the right side of their patients' brains. This put the right side of the brains to sleep for a while. When the patients tried to sing using only the left sides of their brain what did they sound like?

a) They sang beautifully, like trained opera singers.

b) They could open their mouths but no sound came out.

c) They sounded like a calf bellowing.

Teacher's tea-break teaser
A note to the reader:

You try this teaser at your own risk, OK? Don't blame me if you get expelled. To do it all you have to do is sing loudly outside the staff room...

Answer: Words are controlled by the left side of your brain and tunes by the right. When you sing it's hard for your cortex to cope with two sets of information at the same time. I mean – just think, you have to access your memory centres to remember what the words and notes actually sound like. Very musical people actually grow extra neurons in the areas of the right cortex that deal with sound and hearing. OK, got all that? No? Why not ask your brain to chew it over...

Think for yourself (it's not that easy)

1 Thinking is the way that your brain makes sense of the world and organizes the information it gets from your senses. Scientists believe that thinking is a wave of brain activity that spreads as neurons fire signals at each other. Does that get you thinking?

2 The brain has different areas for different jobs like talking or sniffing things, remember. But neurons all over the cortex are involved in thinking and the active areas vary according to what you're doing. Your level of concentration or even your feelings can affect the pattern of brain activity.

3 Brain neurons fire most of the time and scientists think that this could mean your brain is vaguely mulling over past memories. The increased activity caused by thinking might be due to your brain drawing on memories to build up a particular thought.

4 When you do two different things at once (see page 75) each half of your brain has separate thoughts. Is that a good thing? Well, maybe you're in two minds about it.

Bet you never knew!
There is no limit to the number of thoughts you can have. So you don't believe me? Well, read on. Your brain has billions of nerve cells, remember that bit? If you look at a neuron magnified 10,000 times it appears like a tiny tree with over 5,000 branches.

Scientists think there are more than 100,000,000,000 that's ONE HUNDRED BILLION brain synapses. (These are the gaps between neurons, remember.) And scientists believe a thought can travel through these synapses in ANY order. So there may be more possible routes for a thought than atoms in the entire universe. And that means that there's NO LIMIT to the thinking power of your brain.

WOW! That really was something to think about. But oddly enough, although your brain is unbelievably powerful it finds doing several things at once a bit of a strain...

Could you be a scientist?

Some psychologists gave two students a brain-teasing task.

How do you think the students got on?

a) They were useless. The brain simply can't manage to read, talk, listen and write all at the same time.

b) The students found themselves writing the story and repeating out loud the lists the scientists were reading to them.

c) Although the students started off slowly and made mistakes they soon learnt how to do the tasks at the same time.

Answer: c) The brain can be trained to do different things at once. The part that helps you to do this is the cerebellum. And this explains how your hairdresser can cut your hair and chat at the same time without snipping your ears off.

And speaking of talking or talking about speaking the next bit of this chapter will really get your tongue wagging.

Speak for yourself

Try listening to yourself talking and you'll realize that speech is full of hesitation – er ... (sorry, bit of a hesitation there), repetition and mistakes. Yep – speaking is one of the hardest things your brain gets up to. In order to talk properly you've got to...

Access your memory (1) for the correct words and your memory of how to pronounce them.

Use the Broca's area (2) of your cortex to pronounce the words correctly. It should send a message to the bit of the cortex that controls the movement of your vocal cords, tongue and lips to speak the words.

You will need your cerebellum (**3**) to co-ordinate all these complex movements.

BLAH, BLAH, DRONE, WITTER, DRIBBLE...

Use your Wernicke's area (**4**) to put the words in the right grammatical order. (See page 23 for info on how these areas were discovered.)

You will need your ears and the part of the cortex that deals with listen-ing (**5**) to hear your words and the rest of your cortex to check they make sense.

It's (not) that easy! Yet amazingly scientists have found that a good speaker can speak up to three words a second even when someone is mumbling in their ear.

X-RAY VIEW OF TEACHER'S HEAD
(MR CYRIL BELLUM HEAD OF SCIENCE)

Unspeakable speech problems

But, of course, things can still go wrong. Usually at embarrassing moments like when you're talking to someone really famous and important. Here are a few problems that may be caused by the brain...

1 Stupid sayings

This is when you say the right words in the right order but because your cortex hasn't had time to consider the meaning of what you are saying it sounds really stupid. Fast talking sports commentators are particularly good at this. Here's British sports commentator David Coleman:

"THE LATE START IS DUE TO THE TIME"

And US baseball commentator and manager Jerry Coleman:

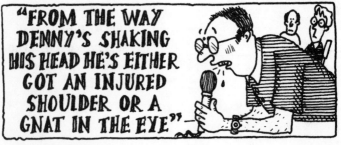

"FROM THE WAY DENNY'S SHAKING HIS HEAD HE'S EITHER GOT AN INJURED SHOULDER OR A GNAT IN THE EYE"

2 Spoonerisms

This means muddling up the first letters or sounds in a series of words. For example, instead of saying, "I have

78

a half-formed wish in my mind," you might accidentally say, "

Usually you wouldn't realize you had made a mistake. It's most likely caused by a fault in the Broca's area (that's the bit of the cortex that deals with speaking words, remember?). Spoonerisms are named after British clergyman Dean William Spooner (1844-1930) who made rather a lot of them.

Bet you never knew!
1 About one in a hundred children suffer from stammering. Stammering is jerky, hesitant speech in which the first sounds of some words are often repeated. Sufferers report that they know what they want to say but they can't say it.
2 Scientists aren't quite sure what causes stammering but it seems to affect boys more than girls and it seems

to be made worse by worry. It's probably linked to a problem in the Broca's area.

3 In the Middle Ages the problem was thought to be due to the tongue not working properly and useless cures were tried such as burning the tongue with a hot iron.

4 Nowadays stammering can be overcome by helping the sufferer to feel more relaxed when talking. Techniques used include learning to speak more slowly and to begin words with a more gentle movement of the lips and tongue.

Bulging brain expressions

Two psychologists are chatting...

Maybe you could ask this LAD to help with your homework?

A whole new language

Sometime in your school career you will have to learn a foreign language. There are about 5,000 languages in the world and they use a huge range of sounds.

For example, some languages in Southern Africa such as Xhosa and Zulu include unusual clicking sounds. Well, whatever languages you learn, once you've learnt to speak the words you then have to learn how to read them. And by some eerie coincidence that's what you're doing right now.

Read all about it

OK, so how are you getting on reading this book? Finding it easy or having a bit of bother with some of the incomprehensible inapprehensible numinous words...

Go on, have a go at remembering them – they're numinous words for bamboozling science teachers.

Scientists reckon that children learn about ten new words a day at school – but that's not such a bad thing because everywhere you look there are written words.

A grown-up who reads a daily paper might get through about 100,000 words every week. This includes all the words they might read in an office job, road signs and even the back of cornflakes packets.

Riveting reading

Reading is great. You can settle down with a good book and forget about the rest of the world. But you won't even reach the end of this sentence without the help of your brain. Here's your chance to discover what your brain is up to when you read. Simply listen in to some more of those fascinating Neuro-phone calls...

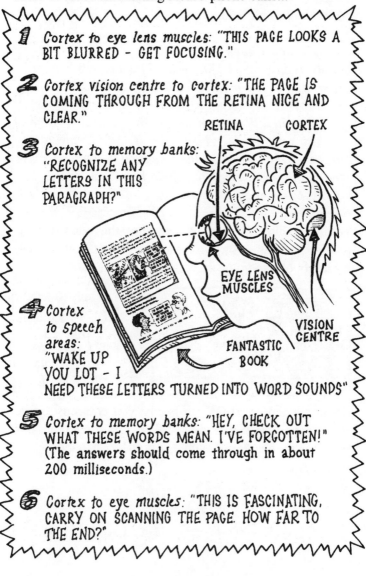

1 Cortex to eye lens muscles: "THIS PAGE LOOKS A BIT BLURRED - GET FOCUSING."

2 Cortex vision centre to cortex: "THE PAGE IS COMING THROUGH FROM THE RETINA NICE AND CLEAR."

RETINA   CORTEX

3 Cortex to memory banks: "RECOGNIZE ANY LETTERS IN THIS PARAGRAPH?"

EYE LENS MUSCLES

4 Cortex to speech areas: "WAKE UP YOU LOT - I NEED THESE LETTERS TURNED INTO WORD SOUNDS"

VISION CENTRE

FANTASTIC BOOK

5 Cortex to memory banks: "HEY, CHECK OUT WHAT THESE WORDS MEAN. I'VE FORGOTTEN!" (The answers should come through in about 200 milliseconds.)

6 Cortex to eye muscles: "THIS IS FASCINATING, CARRY ON SCANNING THE PAGE. HOW FAR TO THE END?"

A note to the reader:

Now ask your brain to move your eyes to the next chunk of text. This should take 30 milliseconds. Hey! Come back you haven't read this bit...

> ***Bet you never knew!***
> *Many really smart kids have difficulty reading. It's often due to a condition called dyslexia (dis-lexy-a). Scientists can't explain what causes dyslexia but there are several different forms of the condition. Some dyslexics see words as back to front or even moving on the page. In one form of the condition the sufferer sees the words on a page but their brain can't turn the words into sounds.*

Teachers think reading is vital, but they don't mean reading for fun – oh no. Teachers expect you to read boring books so you can learn lots of facts.

AND WHEN YOU'VE FINISHED THAT LOT I'LL GIVE YOU SOMETHING INTERESTING

Sounds a real pain? OK, so maybe you could use some really expert scientific advice? Well, better read on, 'cos the next chapter could seriously expand your brainpower...

BEFORE → ← AFTER

LOATHSOME LEARNING

Do you find learning fun? Do you tumble out of bed shouting…

YIPPEE! IT'S SCHOOL TODAY. MORE LOVELY FACTS TO LEARN!

Or do you crawl out of bed thinking...

OH NO, NOT ANOTHER BORING DAY LEARNING STUPID OLD SCIENCE

Well, cheer up! Learning is one of the most vital tasks of your bulging brain and it CAN be fun – but only if you've got something interesting to learn. Like now – so read on.

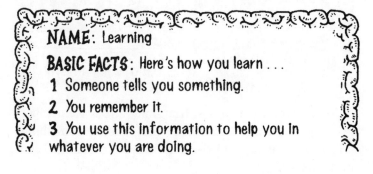

NAME: Learning

BASIC FACTS: Here's how you learn . . .

1 Someone tells you something.

2 You remember it.

3 You use this information to help you in whatever you are doing.

LATE AGAIN, MR JENKINS... I HOPE YOU'VE GOT A NOTE FROM YOUR DAUGHTER

A few facts to learn (and make sure you do)

1 You learn things all the time – not just in school. You learn whenever you notice anything new or try out a new skill.

2 Learning can be nice or nasty:

NICE THINGS TO LEARN: CHOCOLATE ICE-CREAM TASTES YUMMY.

NASTY THING TO LEARN: EAT TOO MUCH AND YOU'LL WANT TO THROW UP.

3 Most people learn by trial and error. Remember learning to ride a bike. But once you've learnt something you can do it effortlessly and without thinking. Like riding that bike.

Teacher's tea-break teaser

Put a fly in your teacher's morning cuppa with this tricky teaser. And remember, if your teacher doesn't believe you – this fact is TRUE. Tap gently on the staffroom door. When it opens, smile brightly and enquire…

IS IT TRUE THAT THERE WERE ONCE PLANS TO INTRODUCE MACHINES TO DO THE JOB OF TEACHERS?

SPLUTTER!

Answer: Yes, in the 1960s US psychologist Burrhus F. Skinner invented a teaching machine called a didak. The machine showed a sentence and you had to complete it. If you got the answer right you got a chance to answer harder questions. Oh goodee! THE GOOD NEWS: The machine never told you off. THE BAD NEWS: It couldn't answer your questions and didn't know how to chat.

Bet you never knew!

It doesn't matter whether they have real teachers or machines to help them – some kids have trouble learning. There are loads of possible reasons for this. Sometimes the difficulties are caused by dyslexia or an eye problem so the child can't read easily. More often the child isn't interested in the lessons. Or perhaps the lessons require skills such as speaking or writing that the child isn't good at. Oddly enough one psychologist who studied how the brain learns suffered learning difficulties as a lad...

Horrible Science Hall of Fame
John B. Watson (1878-1958) Nationality: American

As a boy John B. Watson had a problem with learning. Maybe that's why he was for ever getting into trouble, starting fights and terrorizing his home town in South Carolina, USA.

As he grew older John got mixed up in crime. But when he turned 16 he had a sudden change of heart and started to study really hard at home. He had to study really hard because he had decided to go to university and become a scientist.

But at university John continued to find learning difficult. He couldn't understand his teachers and their boring lectures (sound familiar?).

But he did become fascinated by how rats learn things. Here's what Watson's notebook may have looked like...

The Great Rat Experiment

Today's the BIG day!!! I'm planning to find out if rats can learn from a nasty experience. I've been working hard all week building a three metre long alley for the tests - I call it the "rat-run".

← RAT-RUN   ME

Stage 1

Now to try it out. Will the rat do the obvious and go and grab the food? YES! YES! YES!

The rat runs down the rat-run and grabs the food. Atta boy! This proves that learning happens when you give a rat something new - like the food. This changes the rat's behaviour. Now to test my idea a bit further.

NEXT DAY Stage 2

I've blocked off the rat-run with a thick glass barrier. Will the rat still go down it? Here goes...

Yes - like a streak of lightning and bumped his little nosy on the barrier. Oh dear, poor old ratty. If I'm right the new information about the barrier will change the rat's behaviour - let me see... CRUNCH!

FOOD

NEXT DAY Stage three

I've unblocked the rat-run. Will the rat still run? Maybe he's learnt that he'll get hurt. So he won't take the risk. Yep, he's scared - he's actually turning up his sore little schnozzle at the chance of that lovely food. **NO THANKS!**

Well, that proves my point. Rats can change the way they act by learning from a bad experience.

Hmm - I reckon it's just the same for humans, like me. My old teacher certainly taught me a few nasty lessons. I learnt I'd get a beating if I bunked off school.

Watson's experiments inspired a whole new movement of psychologists called behaviourists who believed that you could help rats – or humans – learn with rewards or punishments. But although Watson was certain that you could learn about human behaviour from studying rats there were squeaks of protest from other scientists when he compared humans to rats...

RATS ARE JUST LIKE US

SQUEAK FOR YOURSELF!

Eventually Watson resigned his university job to go into advertising. Here he put his ideas on learning into practice by selling baby powder. Watson reckoned:

1 Rats chased down the rat-run because they learnt there was food at the end. So by giving the rats a reward you could change their behaviour.

2 You could use advertising to give people the impression that by buying your brand of baby powder they would feel happier and be better parents. This feeling would be a kind of reward. So people would choose to buy your brand.

But did the plan work? What do you think?

a) Watson was sacked after featuring a rat on the advertising posters.

b) Watson's plan failed. People can't be compared to rats. We don't have to feel good when we go shopping.

c) Watson's plan worked and he became a millionaire. His ideas form the basis of modern advertising.

Answer: c) If advertising teaches you that buying a product will improve your life, then you'll probably feel like buying it.

I LOVE MEN WHO SMELL OF PONGY

Are you intelligent?

Are you good at learning things? If so, you may be intelligent. But you might be surprised to know that psychologists don't agree what intelligence is all about. Many, though, believe that intelligence means an ability to solve new problems. Anyway, whatever you call it –

intelligence, being clever, smart or brainy – here's a quick intelligence test to put you through your paces.

True or false?

1 People with small heads aren't as intelligent as people with big heads. This is because people with big heads have bigger brains. TRUE/FALSE

2 As you learn, you develop extra connections between the neurons in their cortex. TRUE/FALSE

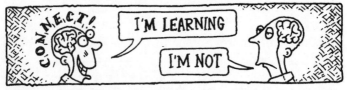

3 Playing lots of computer games can make you more intelligent. TRUE/FALSE

4 Eating fish is good for your brain. TRUE/FALSE

Bulging brain development

Did you know that you learnt half of everything you know in your first five years?

YOU MEAN IT'S TAKEN YOU 75 YEARS TO LEARN THE OTHER HALF, GREAT-GRAN?

In some countries that's before children even start school! Oh, so you don't remember this vital learning period? Well, here's a quick reminder...

The first five years...

0 to six months

When you were born you could breath, suck, swallow and then throw up, dribble, cry, sneeze, cough and stretch. And that's about all because your brain wasn't developed.

DRIBBLE! CRY! ATCHOO! COUGH! STRETCH! THAT'S BETTER

Six months

Your brain had doubled in size. The neurons were growing and branching and forming millions of synapses. You could roll over and smile. You could also copy the expressions on grown-up faces. (Don't try this now – you'll only get told off.)

One year

You had learnt how to pick things up with your hands and you had just spoken your first word. Before then grown-ups probably spoke to you in baby talk and you tried to make the same sounds back. But you hadn't got the hang of the tongue and lip movements so it came out as baby noises. You were just beginning to learn to walk, and falling over quite a lot.

I HATE RUSKS

GOO, GOO GAGA

Two years ...

You could walk run and speak about 274 words. Two vital words you learnt were "wee" and "poo". You were able to recognize the feeling when you had to go and now you could even tell people about it. Soon afterwards you learnt how to use a potty without making an embarrassing mess. And if things went wrong you could take off your underwear without help.

WEEEEE!

Three years

You could speak up to a 1,000 words in short sentences and feed yourself (but not at the same time). You were also learning to draw. Sometimes you were so wrapped up in your drawing or games you might poo or wee in your underwear.
(Hopefully this no longer happens.)

PONG

WELL DONE!

Four years

Your brain was four times bigger than when you were born. You were asking loads of questions using about 1,500 words, and going to the toilet all by yourself.

Five years

You could tell stories and hop and skip and you knew about 2,000 words. And round about this time you started school.

ARGH! SCHOOL!

95

The next few years...

After you turned six, things in your brain got a bit less hectic but the neuron links in your cortex carried on forming. Some time between the ages of six and ten most children learn the following skills:

Tick here

☐ How to play ball games really well.

☐ Reading and joined-up writing.

☐ Writing and telling stories.

☐ Drawing, painting and making models.

☐ Simple cooking and cleaning and even washing up. Oh yes – this is part of growing up, I'm afraid.

☐ Loads of facts and new words at school.

So how far have you got?

Of course not all kids develop at the same speed. Some are late-developers. That doesn't make them stupid – scientific mega-genius Albert Einstein didn't learn to talk until he was four. And girls' and boys' brains develop to different time-tables anyway. For example, for reasons scientists can't quite explain, the parts of the cortex that deal with speech develop earlier in girls than boys. So girls often learn to talk earlier. And boys' and girls' brains go on developing in different ways at different times.

Boys v. girls

Not surprisingly psychologists have found that boys and girls are better at different things...

Bet you never knew!
For example, girls may be better at talking than boys. Oh so you knew this already? Brain scans performed at Yale University School of Medicine, USA, show that men only use the left side of their brains to talk but women use both sides. But who comes out top overall – the battling boys or the gutsy girls?

Read on and find out in...

The battle of the sexes

Scientists have found that boys and girls tend to be better at different things. Of course, you might be different and scientists always argue about the results...

1 One study showed that boys are often quicker at solving tricky maths problems in their heads. Very gifted boys use the right sides of their brains to concentrate on the problem. But girls tend to use both sides and waste time putting their thoughts into words.

2 When boys and girls are given 3-D puzzles to assemble, the boys are better at imagining what the finished puzzle will look like. Once again girls tend to waste time explaining to themselves in words how they will solve the puzzle.

3 But girls' brains are better at controlling their finger movements for delicate fiddly tasks. So the girls might well be quicker at putting the puzzle together.

4 Boys tend to have a good sense of direction. They are very good at building up a clear idea of a route in the right side of their brains.

5 But they're not so good at remembering landmarks. Girls with their better memory for words can remember the landmarks even if they're sometimes less sure about the direction.

Important note: In conclusion, every scientific study has found that boys and girls have differing abilities in some areas and use their brains in different ways. But, and here's the important bit, OVERALL, THEY ARE EQUALLY CLEVER. So shut it, OK?

And there you have it. Learning is a vital function of your bulging brain. Now, have you learnt everything in this chapter? Well, one thing's for certain – you won't have learnt anything without a memory. Luckily, the next mind-expanding chapter can help you. And you'll soon find those memories flooding back...

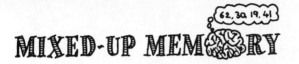

MIXED-UP MEMORY

Welcome to this unforgettable chapter. It's about memory. Just what is this mysterious ability? And how does it work? And will you remember anything after you've read this book? Er ... now what was I talking about?

Bulging fact file

NAME: Memory

BASIC FACTS: Memory works like this ...

1 You sense something.

2 You put it in your memory.

3 You can recall the memory when something reminds you of it. The reminder might be a word, an event or even a smell.

DISGUSTING DETAILS: You've got not one but *three* memories.

1 Short term memory. Useful for phone numbers, etc. You forget these memories in 30 seconds. Some kids store their science knowledge in here.

...BUT I JUST TOLD YOU ABOUT SHORT TERM MEMORY!

THAT WAS 40 SECONDS AGO, MISS

...OF COURSE CHALKY ONLY TOOK ONE SUGAR IN HIS TEA - IT WAS HARD STUFF TO GET HOLD OF SEVENTY YEARS AGO

2 Long term memory. This is stuff you remember for years. It's where Grandpa stores all those boring old yarns of life when he was a lad. These first two memory systems are based in your cortex.

3 A special memory for skills like riding a bike that you can use without being aware of having to remember them. This memory seems to be based in your cerebellum.

IT'S ALL THANKS TO YOUR CEREBELLUM

SARAH BELLUM - WHO'S SHE?

Mysterious long-term memory-makers

Two areas deep in the cortex, the thalamus and the hippocampus (hippo-camp-us), help create longer-term memory. People with injuries to the thalamus have difficulty in remembering the injury. And in 1953 an American man had the hippocampus on both sides of his brain removed. This was intended to stop fits caused by uncontrollable neuron firing. The fits stopped. But although the man can recall old memories from before the operation, he can't remember anything that's happened since then.

Bet you never knew!
Older people also suffer from this problem. And this, too, seems to be linked to damage to the hippocampus. From the age of about 30 the neurons in this region begin to die off and by the time a person reaches extreme old age they've lost about 30 per cent. Although scientists aren't too sure why this process takes place, the effects on the memory are fairly obvious. Perhaps some of your more mature teachers are already suffering from the effects.

Hopefully your memory is much better? Well, let's pick up the Neuro-phone and check out how it works...

A memorable joke

The brain is about to try and remember a joke...

MY DOG HAS NO NOSE

HOW DOES IT SMELL?

TERRIBLE!

(OK, I didn't say the joke was any good.)

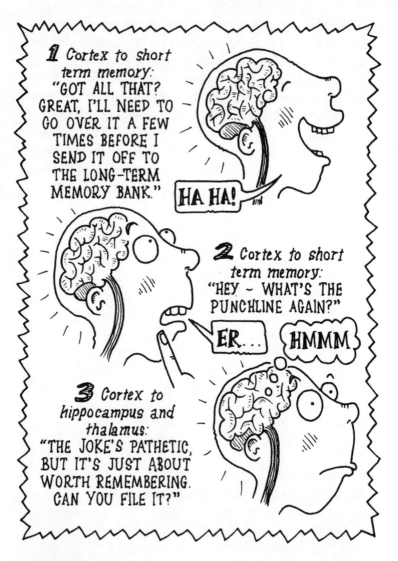

Scientific note

Scientists aren't quite sure how this happens. It seems to involve a change in neuron chemistry. This makes it easier to send a message along a particular route through the maze of neurons in your cortex. (Each neuron pathway is storing a particular part of a memory. Some store colours and others can store shapes.) The memory of the joke should remain in your brain even if you can't recall it. People call this "sub-conscious memory".

A few weeks later...

4 Cortex to *memory banks*: "GOT THAT JOKE ABOUT THE DOG FILED? I WAS JUST WONDERING WHERE I HEARD IT."

5 *Memory banks*: "YEAH, IT'S HERE. I'LL JUST CHECK ITS SOURCE... DON'T YOU REMEMBER, IT WAS IN THAT *BULGING BRAINS* BOOK."

6 *Cortex*: "BLIMEY, SO IT WAS!"

No doubt you'll be pleased to hear there's room in your memory for lots more jokes (and other stuff). Remember all those billions of neurons and synapses in your cortex? Well, scientists reckon you can squeeze facts in your memory to fill 20,000 encyclopaedias. Do that and your brain really would be bulging. You might even win a memory competition...

The Horrible Science memory competition

This competition is unforgettable. All the prize winners have shown powers of recollection that will live long in our memories.

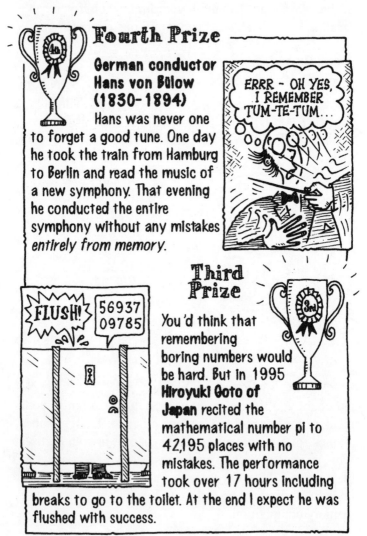

Fourth Prize

German conductor Hans von Bülow (1830–1894)

Hans was never one to forget a good tune. One day he took the train from Hamburg to Berlin and read the music of a new symphony. That evening he conducted the entire symphony without any mistakes *entirely from memory.*

ERRR – OH YES, I REMEMBER TUM-TE-TUM...

Third Prize

FLUSH!

56937 09785

You'd think that remembering boring numbers would be hard. But in 1995 **Hiroyuki Goto of Japan** recited the mathematical number pi to 42,195 places with no mistakes. The performance took over 17 hours including breaks to go to the toilet. At the end I expect he was flushed with success.

Second Prize

Devout **Mehmed Ali Halici of Turkey** recited 6,666 verses of religious text in 1967. Could you do that in your school assembly? Come to think of it would you fancy an assembly that was 18 hours long?

BLAH BLAH

AND NOW FOR VERSE 3772...

First Prize

I WILL NOW RECITE THE ENTIRE BIBLE... IN LATIN

Goes to **Russian Solomon Veniaminoff.** Solomon wanted to be a violinist but an ear disease slightly damaged his hearing. In the 1930s he decided to become a journalist. Later he worked as a stage entertainer where he wowed the crowds with his unforgettable talent for remembering incredibly long numbers or lists of words. From time to time he also helped psychologist Alexander Luria (1902-1977) with his work on memory. Here's Solomon's story. Of course, we can't remember the exact details but this story is based on the real facts...

The man who never forgot

Moscow, May 1928

The slender young man was clearly on edge. "My name is Solomon," he stammered. "My editor sent me to see you because of my memory."

"What's wrong with it?" asked Alexander Luria curiously as he leaned back in his rocking-chair. Solomon nervously swept his black hair from his eyes.

"People say that I have an exceptional memory. The fact is I can remember every single thing that has happened to me since I was one year old."

"Fascinating but unlikely," smiled Luria. There was an uncomfortable silence broken only by the ticking of the large old clock on the mantelpiece. Then Luria sighed.

"Oh well, I suppose we'd better test you. I'd like you to try to remember this sequence of numbers."

The scientist quickly jotted down a series of 30 numbers and then read them out to the young man.

Solomon looked even more worried and gazed briefly into nothing. His dark, dreamy eyes seemed fixed on a distant object that Luria couldn't see.

Then he repeated the numbers perfectly.

The scientist's mouth dropped open. "But that's astounding!" he gasped.

"I could say them backwards if you like," said Solomon quietly. And he gave a shy, fleeting smile.

1958

Thirty years later Alexander Luria sat in the warm sunshine gazing vacantly at his garden. He was lost in thought and as usual he felt rather tired. In front of him lay a pile of old papers covered in his spidery handwriting. The paper was crinkled and yellow with age.

"So how do I turn all this into a book?" he mused to himself. "Where to begin, that's the first problem."

"Why not begin at the beginning?" said a voice. Luria looked up in surprise at the man sitting quietly in the corner. The visitor's hair was grey with age and his figure was stooped and thick-set.

"Oh, Solomon I'm so sorry, I quite forgot you were here. Now what were we saying?"

"We were discussing the book you were going to write about memory and our 30 years of working together. That's why you invited me here at 4.24 p.m. yesterday."

"Has it really been that long?" asked the scientist wearily.

"Well, on and off, when I wasn't working on the stage."

"I think I'll begin my book on that day in June, when

was it? 1929 when you first came to see me."

"It was 1928," said Solomon firmly, "and the month was May. I remember you in your grey suit sitting in your rocking-chair. And that old-fashioned clock you had. And then those 30 numbers ... what were they now? 62, 30, 19, 41..."

Luria gazed in growing shock at the first page of his yellowing notes. Yes, there in his own handwriting was the exact sequence of numbers repeated with eerie accuracy over a gap of 30 years.

"But that's astounding!" he wheezed breathlessly.

"That's what you said at the time," said Solomon with his familiar shy smile.

"But you must have remembered millions of pieces of information since then. You're a lucky man Solomon, I do admire this gift of yours."

"It's no gift!" exclaimed Solomon bitterly. "As I told you in 1929 it's a curse. I often wished I could forget things. Sometimes all these facts and numbers and lists jostle in my mind like a huge crowd – like words in poetry or sparks in a fireworks display. They drive me crazy! The greatest gift is to forget things. But that's one gift I will never possess. Forgetting is a wonderful thing."

And his eyes sparkled with tears.

Solomon's secret

After years of patient study Luria figured out the secret of Solomon Veniaminoff's astonishing memory. It was due to the way his mind worked. Solomon suffered from a disease called synaesthesia (sin-ees-thees-ia). Incredible though it sounds this rare brain disease made Solomon experience sounds as colours. He told one psychologist...

WHAT A CRUMBLY YELLOW VOICE YOU HAVE!

By remembering the colours he saw when hearing things and by imagining numbers as people he found it easy to remember tons of information. But the only way he could ever forget something was to imagine it was written on paper and he was burning it.

Boost your memory

Would you want a memory like Solomon's? Probably not – but with a more powerful memory you could get top marks in your science tests every time and even remember your dad's birthday. The good news is you don't need a special brain to develop an excellent memory.

Bet you never knew!
One painful way to improve your memory is to stick electrodes into your brain. Experiments in the 1900s by surgeon Wilder Penfield in Canada found this gives you vivid flashbacks from your past. I expect some of them proved a bit shocking.

Picture this...

But don't worry, there are many less painful methods of improving your memory. Here's one of them. Supposing tomorrow you have a science test and you need to remember to feed the goldfish and take your sandwiches to school.

1 *Try* to remember to do these things. This should store the information in your short-term memory.

2 For reasons that scientists don't quite understand you can remember pictures better than facts. It might be because you can link pictures with other memories more easily and in some way this makes them easier to recall. So make up a mental picture to help you remember. For example, you could imagine your teacher eating a goldfish in a sandwich.

3 When you get up the next morning and get ready for school, the thought of facing your teacher again will immediately make you remember the image of her eating a goldfish sandwich. So you use your teacher as a memory cue – that's a kind of clue to help you remember the goldfish, the sandwiches and the test, stupid.

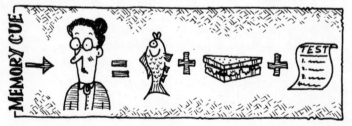

Terror in the air

Your memory can be affected by your feelings. In the 1950s Mitchell Berkun, a scientist working for the US Army, dreamt up this horrible experiment.

1 Take a group of army recruits up in a plane.

2 Right, you guys. Here's the emergency drill. Make sure you listen good and proper. There's 12 steps to remember. Your life may depend on getting them right.

3 ...and finally item 12. You inflate your life-jacket by pulling the cord. Got all that?

Er, I think so.

4 What are those fire engines doing on the ground?

5 Hey, the engine's just cut out!

6 We're going to crash!

7 Right who can remember their emergency drill? What's step one?

I want my mummy!

Where's the sick bag?

Of course, the whole incident including the fire engines on the ground had been set up by Berkun. The terrible test showed that the recruits could only remember half the instructions when they were scared out of their wits.

And talking about feelings ... the next chapter's all about them – the highs, the lows, the excitement and the horror. So, do you feel like reading a bit further?

FORCEFUL FEELINGS

Are you a touchy-feely person who is always laughing or weeping? Do you pride yourself on being the strong, silent type? Well, whatever you're like on the surface, your brain is bulging with powerful feelings.

Feeling the force

Scientists claim there are six types of emotion that people feel all over the world. Huh – what do they know? When was the last time you saw an emotional scientist? Well, we've managed to find one and photograph the full range of his six emotions.

Of course, feelings can get horribly mixed up. That's why people cry when they're happy or sometimes feel a bit down after some good news.

Scientists have scarcely begun to explain why our emotions get so tangled. However, as you're about to discover, emotions can be triggered by several different chemicals. With so many of these chemicals sloshing about at the same time it wouldn't be surprising if your brain got some mixed messages.

Complicated feelings

Feeling emotion is actually more complicated than you might think. For one thing you need to co-ordinate three areas of your brain. And that really gets the Neuro-phone lines buzzing. Just listen to this: Your teacher is telling you off...

Scientific note:
Dopamine (dope-a-mean) is a chemical that seems to make your neurons more active and fire more signals. Obviously the emotion you feel depends on what's going on. It could be terror or joy or anything in between.

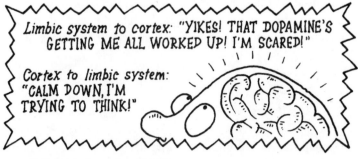

Limbic system to cortex: "YIKES! THAT DOPAMINE'S GETTING ME ALL WORKED UP! I'M SCARED!"

Cortex to limbic system: "CALM DOWN, I'M TRYING TO THINK!"

Bulging brain expressions
One neurologist says to another...

IS YOUR WORK INTERESTING?

WELL MY **RAS** IS FIRED UP!

Is that some kind of stove?

Answer: No. The reticular (ret-tick-u-lar) activating system or RAS for short is the area in the brain stem that makes the dopamine. By the way, you might be interested to know that in small kids the RAS is easily switched on and that's why they get so easily scared. As you grow up the RAS quietens down because your cortex learns when there's a real monster and when it's just a curtain blowing in a darkened room.

117

Dizzy dopamine v. serious serotonin

So dopamine shakes up your limbic system and you feel emotion. But you don't always do what you feel like doing. That's because of another brain chemical called serotonin (seer-ro-tone-in). This is squirted by neurons linking the limbic system and the cortex. Serotonin tends to calm the neurons down and makes you feel more sensible. (It can also make you feel happy and relaxed.)

Imagine you've guzzled some lovely cream buns and you're greedily eyeing up the rest.

In other words serotonin tells you *not* to do things. It's like having a sensible teacher stuck between your ears. (Now that *is* a scary thought!)

By now you might be wondering why your cortex needs to get involved in feelings. After all, you feel things in the limbic system and you've got dizzy dopamine to get you all worked up and serious serotonin to calm you down. Well, the cortex is there to think things over and make the ultimate decision...

And of course, getting your cortex involved helps you stop to think when you get emotional. This can help you control your temper.

Bet you never knew!
Scientists believe that people with low levels of serotonin can become bad-tempered or even violent. That's because they find it harder to control their feelings. And talking about uncontrollable feelings...

HORRIBLE SCIENCE HEALTH WARNING
There's a feeling of TERROR lurking just over the page.

Fear and fury

Although feelings are controlled and felt in your brain, your body also joins in and helps you to feel emotions. Sometimes in a horrible way. Just imagine you haven't done your homework for the third time running: your teacher is seething. Never mind, here's your chance to make interesting scientific observations on the effect of anger and fear...

An angry teacher

ADRENAL GLANDS OVER KIDNEYS SQUIRTING A HORMONE CALLED ADRENALINE (AD-REN-A-LIN) INTO THE BLOOD. THIS CAUSES ALL THE OTHER EFFECTS...

WILKINS, I WANT A WORD WITH YOU...

Stored sugar pouring out of liver into blood and on its way to feed the raging brain

Lungs panting in air – ten times more than usual

Adrenal glands

Digestion stopped

Fat being dissolved and sent to the muscles to provide energy for violent physical action. (This might sound a bit extreme for a teacher but remember those bodily reactions developed millions of years ago to help early people fight woolly mammoths and other fierce creatures.)

Did someone mention scientific observations? Well, maybe you're not in the mood. Inside you might be feeling a bit wobbly, petrified even. Maybe a bit like this...

A scared child

ADRENAL GLANDS ALSO PUMPING OUT ADRENALINE – BUT IN ADDITION...

Hair standing on end*

Eyes closed*

Shoulders drawn up*

YES, SIR

Body bent*

Kneecaps buckle*

*These are all part of a reflex action called startle reflex. By bending your body you're protecting your vital organs just in case your teacher decides to give you a violent kick. (Hopefully he won't go that far, but this is another primitive reaction which was a very useful protection against those woolly mammoths.)

Important note:

Oh no! Your teacher's figured out it was you who absent-mindedly left chewing gum on his chair. Oh-er, you're going to cop it now. TAKE COVER! YOUR TEACHER IS ABOUT TO GO BALLISTIC...

A teacher who is just about to explode

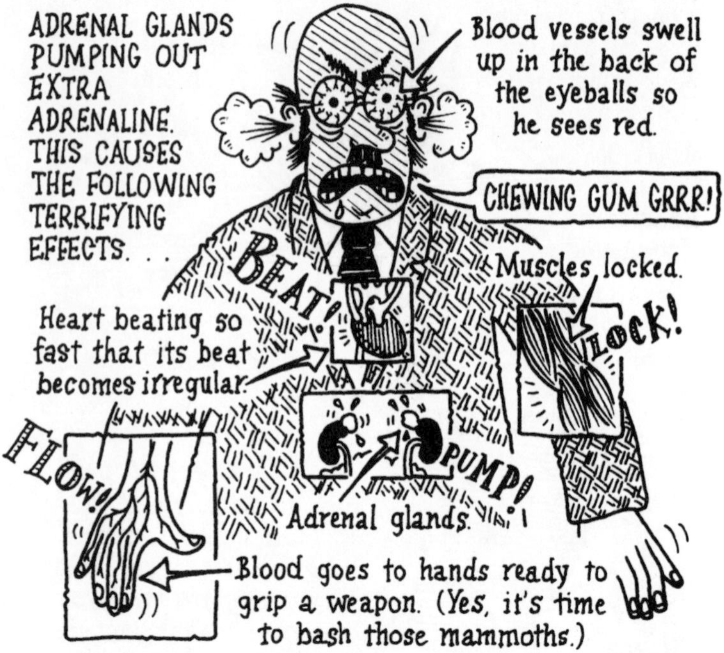

ADRENAL GLANDS PUMPING OUT EXTRA ADRENALINE. THIS CAUSES THE FOLLOWING TERRIFYING EFFECTS...

Blood vessels swell up in the back of the eyeballs so he sees red.

CHEWING GUM GRRR!

BEAT!

Muscles locked.

LOCK!

Heart beating so fast that its beat becomes irregular.

FLOW!

PUMP!

Adrenal glands.

Blood goes to hands ready to grip a weapon. (Yes, it's time to bash those mammoths.)

An even more scared child

White face. (Blood drains out of the skin so that any wounds you get won't bleed too much. Another sensible Stone Age precaution.)

Spit dries up. GULP!

JIBBER TREMBLE!

THUMP! THUMP!

Heart speeds up.

122

The long, long, long wait outside the head teacher's room

So you've been sent for a little chat with the head teacher? Oh dear, this could prove painful. Here are a few things to think about whilst you're waiting for the axe to fall...

Four fearful feelings facts

1 You feel stress. This is the fear you feel when you're scared but you can't run away. Well, you can but they'll only catch you and then you'll really catch it. Some kids feel stress when they start a new school and some feel it every day they go to school.

2 Chewing your fingernails yet? Masticating keratin* is a common response to stress.

*(Mas-tic-kate-ing) = posh term for chewing. (Ker-rat-in) = the substance your nails are made of.

Scientists think that people feel more cheerful when they chew things. It's healthier to chew gum (sugar-free, of course) but that's what got you into this mess. By the way, when you're stressed-out your sense of taste stops working. So the gum would taste like someone's already chewed it.

3 Your adrenal glands are squirting a hormone called cortisone (cor-ti-zone). The aim of this chemical is to prepare your muscles for action later on. Sugar pours into your blood, your brain feels more alert because it's getting more sugar and the nerves are firing like crazy. But you feel rotten – all nervy and jittery. Yikes!

4 You'd better apologize to the head teacher – you might even be let off without a punishment. But there's one feeling that's even worse than being stressed. It's worse because it makes you feel really miserable, really sad. It can spoil your whole life...

Bet you never knew!

Depression is a brain condition that makes you so miserable you want to go to bed and cry and stay there for ever. Scientists think it may be the result of a shortage of brain chemicals such as serotonin. If you ever feel this way try taking a deep breath. Let it out slowly and relax. Yep, that's it: for some reason relaxing actually helps you feel better. Remember this rotten scary fearful miserable feeling is caused by a few chemicals in your bulging brain.

The secret of happiness

For hundreds of years people have searched for this elusive secret and got very uptight and miserable because they couldn't find it. But it's here, here in this very book! Ahem, wait for it... This next bit is based on research by US psychologists Paul Costa and Robert McRae. In the 1970s, Costa and McRae interviewed large numbers of different people and tried to discover what it was in their personalities that made them happy or sad. Here's what they found: to be happy it helps if you enjoy meeting new people.

Don't expect too much from life. That way good things come as a pleasant surprise.

But always look for the bright side of every situation.

And if you can't find happiness by using these simple techniques then don't worry. Science has found ways of making you cheer up whether you like it or not...

Bet you never knew!

1 *In the 1950s it was common to treat diseases of the mind by cutting the nerves to the front part of the cortex. This made the patient less emotional (maybe that's because it's hard to be emotional when you've got a thumping headache).*

2 *US surgeon Walter Freeman invented his own version of this horrible treatment. Walt stuck an ice-pick through a patient's eye-socket into the brain and cut the nerves that way. I expect he only wanted to pick their brains, ha-ha. Hardened doctors were known to swoon at this revolting spectacle. The patients also felt sick and confused afterwards.*

3 *In 1963 scientist RG Heath tried a new technique to control feelings. He stuck electrodes in the brain of a man with a brain disease that caused uncontrollable rages. By pressing buttons the man gave electric shocks to different areas of his brain.*

But you don't have to drill holes in your skull or wield ice-picks or even suffer electric shocks to feel emotional. Try tuning into your favourite music. Yep, why not enjoy the feel-good factor with our exclusive relaxation tapes...?

The Horrible Science ♫ Feel-good Tapes ♫

Recorded by Austrian psychologist Manfried Klein...

SPONSORED BY SOOTHIE-BONCE HEADACHE TABLETS.

Chill out to the brain calming tones of musical gems such as "The Brandenberg Concertos" by German composer JS Bach (1685-1750)

BEFORE   AFTER

IMPORTANT NOTE:

Yeah, it's dead boring classical stuff by an even more dead composer. But Klein found that people all over the world go gooey when they listen to it. Yes, even people like you who think classical music is best enjoyed by zombies and elderly teachers. So get in the groove, chill out and feel mellow...

Could you be a scientist?

The situation you're in and the reactions of other people can affect the way you feel. Sounds common sense, doesn't it? But psychologists have tried to find out precisely how important these factors are. And they've dreamt up a few brain-boggling experiments...

1 In the late 1960s two psychologists from New York University, USA, played frisbee in the waiting-room of Grand Central station. They laughed and joked and got in the way. After a while they threw the frisbee to a third scientist who was pretending to be a stranger. She joined in the game. What happened next?

a) Other people joined in the game.

b) Everyone ignored the frisbee players.

c) The scientists were arrested for causing a nuisance.

2 The same team put three people in a room and gave them forms to fill in. Then they wafted smoke through vents to make it look like the room was on fire. Two of the people were actually psychologists in disguise and they ignored the smoke. What did the third person do?

a) Ran about shouting…

b) Ignored the smoke.

c) Got a fire extinguisher and squirted the scientists with foam from head to foot.

3 US psychologist Philip Zimbardo set up a tasteless experiment. A nice, friendly scientist was given the job of persuading complete strangers to eat fried grasshoppers.

Next, another scientist rudely ordered people to eat the insects. What did the results show?

a) People were more likely to eat the grasshoppers when they were asked nicely.

b) The test was scrapped when someone threw up. This is odd because grasshoppers are a delicacy in parts of Africa such as Morocco. They have a lovely crunchy texture and taste like dried shrimp.

c) People ate the grasshoppers on both occasions. But they said they felt different when they were ordered to eat them.

Mind you, there's one situation where you'd feel nothing. It's when you get knocked out cold by a bash on the head. And if you want to find out what it does to your brain take a look at the next chapter. It's a real knockout.

FASCINATING!

130

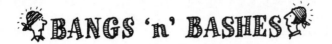

As you've probably realized by now, the brain is an intricate and delicate bit of equipment. So, not surprisingly, a bash on the head can damage the brain in all sorts of horrible and unexpected ways. Luckily, you do have a bit of natural protection.

Bulging brain protection
Your bulging brain is naturally well protected. Let's take a look at this CAT scan.

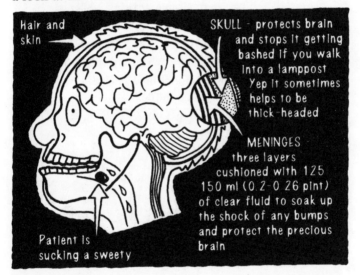

Hair and skin →

SKULL - protects brain and stops it getting bashed if you walk into a lamppost Yep it sometimes helps to be thick-headed

MENINGES three layers cushioned with 125 150 ml (0.2-0.26 pint) of clear fluid to soak up the shock of any bumps and protect the precious brain

Patient is sucking a sweety

A nasty blow
Despite these elaborate defences a bash on the bonce can make you lose your memory – or cause amnesia to use the scientific term. In this state you can't remember what hit you, or even that you've been hit. And you may lose consciousness. And consciousness is actually the most incredible thing your bulging brain gets up to...

Bulging fact file

NAME : Consciousness

BASIC FACTS : It means being aware of your thoughts and feelings. Scientists aren't too sure how this happens. The whole of your cortex seems to be involved in making you aware of your thoughts and what they mean.

DISGUSTING DETAILS : It's possible to run around and perform simple actions whilst unconscious. In the 1956 FA Cup Final goalkeeper Bert Trautmann was knocked unconscious in a collision with an opposing player. But battling Bert somehow made a vital save and completed the game.

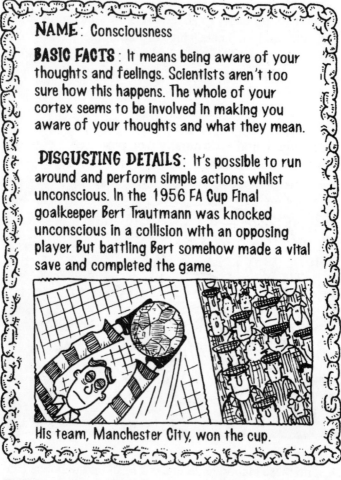

His team, Manchester City, won the cup.

Bulging brain bumps

Here are some vital facts to bump up your knowledge.

1 When you get up in the morning your brain gets a rude awakening. As you lift your head up your brain slops forward and bangs against the front part of your skull.

Luckily your meninges and the fluid around the brain stop it getting too battered.

FLUID

WOBBLE!

BRAIN WOBBLES LIKE A JELLY

2 Some neurologists think the shock makes some people feel bad-tempered in the morning. (It's either that or the sour milk in their tea.)

WHAT D'YOU THINK YOU'RE STARING AT?

3 In car crashes the effect of the brain being thrown forwards is far more damaging than a blow on the head. The shock is more likely to tear blood vessels and the brain itself, leaving wounds that cannot easily be treated because they're inside the skull.

4 The effects of an injury can depend on which part of the cortex gets damaged. It can lead to problems reading, smelling or tasting, or amnesia – that's loss of memory, remember?

THANKS – WHO ARE YOU?

25th WEDDING

5 In 1997 Vicky, a ten-year-old British girl, banged her head and started writing backwards and upside-down. Vicky could read her own writing but it must have baffled her teacher. A year later she got overexcited watching football and banged her head again. The next day, for reasons that neurologists can't explain, her writing had returned to normal.

Bet you never knew!
In 1998 a retired Scottish footballer said that his memory loss was due to heading the ball too much. His wife said that he often chatted to his grandchildren and then forgot whom he was talking to. Before the 1950s, footballs were made of heavy leather and when it rained they sucked in water and got heavier. If they hit you on the head they could knock you out.

HORRIBLE HEALTH WARNING!

So let that be a warning. Don't go bashing your head against hard solid objects such as brick walls, floors or teachers. It's horribly unhealthy.

BRICK WALL: HARD SOLID OBJECT

HEAD: NOT SUCH A HARD SOLID OBJECT

Bulging fact file

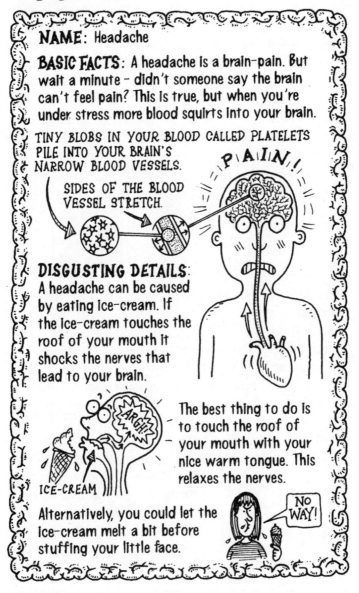

NAME: Headache

BASIC FACTS: A headache is a brain-pain. But wait a minute – didn't someone say the brain can't feel pain? This is true, but when you're under stress more blood squirts into your brain.

TINY BLOBS IN YOUR BLOOD CALLED PLATELETS PILE INTO YOUR BRAIN'S NARROW BLOOD VESSELS.

P A I N !

SIDES OF THE BLOOD VESSEL STRETCH.

DISGUSTING DETAILS: A headache can be caused by eating ice-cream. If the ice-cream touches the roof of your mouth it shocks the nerves that lead to your brain.

ARGH

ICE-CREAM

The best thing to do is to touch the roof of your mouth with your nice warm tongue. This relaxes the nerves.

Alternatively, you could let the ice-cream melt a bit before stuffing your little face.

NO WAY!

Teacher's tea-break teaser

To succeed in this teaser you need split-second timing, oodles of charm and skin like a rhinoceros. All you do is choose a morning when your teacher has been teaching an extra-difficult class. He'll probably have a headache and will be gulping down a few painkillers with his tea.

Tap quietly on the staff-room door (remember teachers have feelings too). When the door opens your teacher will be looking grim. So smile sweetly and enquire...

DOES FROWNING MAKE YOUR HEADACHE WORSE?

Answer: Yes, it does and here's why. By frowning you squeeze several kilometres of blood vessels in your head. This squashes the platelets and makes the pain more intense. The best thing to do with a headache is to relax and try to feel happy. When you smile the blood vessels relax and your headache should ease.

Ahh, that's better!

Horrible headache cures

And that's a lot better than the ancient Roman treatment for a headache. Roman doctor Scribonius Largus recommended whacking the patient on the head with an electric fish. This fishy shock treatment was supposed to cure the ache. It didn't. Mind you, if you lived in the Stone Age there weren't any of those nice painkillers or even an electric fish around.

Stone age brain surgery

1 Take a sharp bit of flint.

2 Scrape the hair and skin off the patient's head.

3 Ignore any screams from the victim, sorry patient.

4 Carry on until a hole appears in the skull.

No one is sure why this operation was carried out in the Stone Age but it was used in ancient Greece to tackle persistent headaches. Although it didn't do much good the victims often survived with their brains bulging out of the gory hole. Stone Age skulls have been found in which the skull had started to heal.

Actually this treatment – known today as trepanning (trep-panning) – is still performed by surgeons. You'll be relieved to know they use modern instruments rather than lumps of rock. It's done in an emergency to relieve a build-up of blood pressure in the brain caused by a blood clot. And, as you now know, people can survive with a hole in the bonce. A person can even survive with a hole made by an accident.

Groaning Gage

Everyone liked Phineas Gage of Vermont, USA. The young railway foreman was a lively and happy-go-lucky chap. Until one day in 1848...

Phin was blasting a path for a new railway. He was trying to push some dynamite down a hole using an iron bar. When disaster struck...

The dynamite blew up and the iron bar shot straight through Phin's head. The bar was found a few metres away spattered with bits of poor Phin's brains.

Phin was knocked out by the blow but quickly came

round and even managed to walk to the doctor's. The hole was big enough for the doctor to put his fingers inside Phin's skull...

Amazingly, Phin lived – although he was ill for a few weeks. But as a result of his injuries he was a changed man. He was moody, foul-mouthed, rude and often drunk.

He lost jobs frequently, but his wits remained sharp. He made money by exhibiting himself in fairs with the iron bar stuck through his head.

Scientists were eager to study Phin's battered bonce. So he sold his body to *several* medical schools for cash up front.

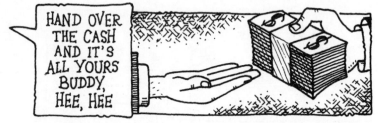

After Phin's death the medical schools argued over who owned the body and, of course, the brain. The doctors were keen to remove Phin's brain and look at the damage.

The doctors found that Phin's brain hadn't been able to repair the damage it suffered. The damaged front cortex area wasn't vital for life but it had clearly shaped Phin's personality.

The famous iron bar ended up in the museum at Harvard Medical College. Hope they cleaned it up first.

But you don't need a near-fatal brain injury to lose consciousness. No, in fact you do it far less painfully every night when you curl up your tootsies and snuggle down in your nice warm bed. And if that's where you are right now why not take a peek at the next chapter? It's a real dream.

Or is it a nightmare?

NASTY NIGHTMARES

This chapter is about sleep. It's about dreams and it's about nightmares...

Warning to sensitive readers: Are you easily scared and reading this chapter in bed? Well, if you must scream, scream quietly.

But, try not to be too petrified – nightmares and dreams are fascinating effects made by your bulging brain in the middle of sleep. Here are a few more facts to sleep on...

Bulging fact file

NAME: Sleep

BASIC FACTS: When you go to sleep you lose consciousness. Your sleeping brain produces delta brainwaves (see page 41) and you're unaware of your surroundings. Oh, so you knew that already? Well try and stay awake for the next bit.

DISGUSTING DETAILS: Staying awake for two weeks can kill you. Scientists believe that the body needs a period of rest each day. Without it, the body gets more and more exhausted and vital functions like heartbeat begin to falter.

BEAT...
BEAT...
...ZZZ

TIRED TEACHER

So sleep is good for you. And whilst you're lying in bed you can always listen in to those chattering Neuro-phone wires as your brain tries to help you to nod off...

Sleepy signals

Cortex to all brain areas: "I'M REALLY WIDE AWAKE. DO I HAVE TO GO TO SLEEP?"

Pineal gland to cortex: "NIGHT-NIGHT, CORTEX. SOME OF THIS NICE MELATONIN WILL CALM YOU DOWN"

SCIENTIFIC NOTE
Melatonin (mel-a tone-in) damps down the activity in the cortex. The pineal gland pumps out melatonin every night on a 24-hour cycle.

Cortex: "YAWN, I'M FEELING REALLY SLEEPY."

RAS* to cortex: "COME ON, CORTEX, TIME YOU WERE TUCKED UP. HERE'S SOME NICE SEROTONIN** TO HELP YOU SLEEP."

SCIENTIFIC NOTE
At this point your brain should lose consciousness. But you won't notice that bit. Why? Because you'll be asleep, too, stupid.

Cortex: "Zzzz."

* That's the reticular activating system in your brain stem, remember.

** That's the "sensible" chemical that damps down your feelings. The serotonin should calm your cortex down even more.

Bulging brain expressions

Two psychologists are chatting.

Is this dangerous?

Answer: No, but it's annoying for everyone else. Somniloquy (som-nil-o-kwee) means talking in your sleep. Somnambulism (som-nam-bew-lis-m) means walking in your sleep. So the psychologist walks and talks in his sleep. Well, could be worse: in 1993 a British businessman had to be rescued by fire-fighters after falling into a rubbish chute. He had fallen in whilst sleepwalking in the nude.

Spot the sleepwalker

One in twenty children walk in their sleep and some adults do this when they're feeling stressed. Does your mum/dad/brother/sister/hamster sleepwalk? Here are a few signs to look out for.

A SLEEPWALKING TEACHER

EYES OPEN BUT ASLEEP

BLANK EXPRESSION

mumble, mumble

ER... THE LESS SAID ABOUT THIS THE BETTER

TALKING GIBBERISH

Mind you, some teachers act this way on a Monday morning when they are supposedly awake.

Bet you never knew!
It's quite harmless to wake a sleepwalker but it's a good idea to do it gently. After all, it's a bit confusing for someone to wake up suddenly and find themselves out of bed. On waking up, the sleepwalking person can't remember where they've been. So break the news gently, OK?

A bit of an eye-opener

Any sleep, even with a bit of sleepwalking thrown in, is better than no sleep at all. In the 1960s scientists kept volunteers awake to measure the effects of lack of sleep on their brains and bodies. What you are about to read is a story based on real events that happened in these tests. So try to keep awake for the next few minutes...

Don't try this experiment at home. You might keep parents awake and this can have a magical shrinking effect on pocket money. And, as you are about to find out, losing too much sleep is very unhealthy. For this reason scientists are no longer keen to perform this experiment.

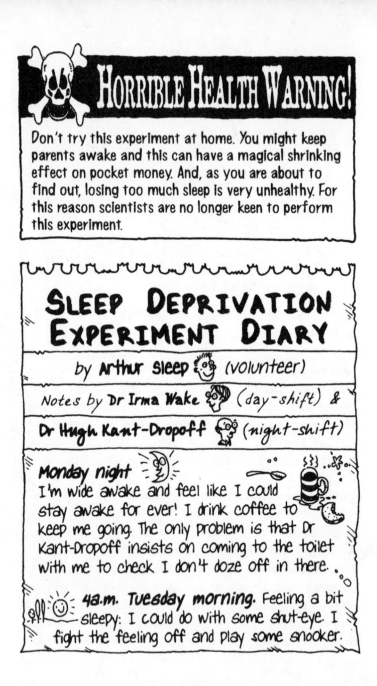

SLEEP DEPRIVATION EXPERIMENT DIARY

by **Arthur Sleep** (volunteer)

Notes by **Dr Irma Wake** (day-shift) &

Dr Hugh Kant-Dropoff (night-shift)

Monday night
I'm wide awake and feel like I could stay awake for ever! I drink coffee to keep me going. The only problem is that Dr Kant-Dropoff insists on coming to the toilet with me to check I don't doze off in there.

4a.m. Tuesday morning. Feeling a bit sleepy: I could do with some shut-eye. I fight the feeling off and play some snooker.

TUESDAY MORNING
Dr Kant-Dropoff writes. . .

Arthur is fine. His heartbeat and reflexes are normal. I wired him up to an EEG machine and his brainwaves are normal. I'm a bit sleepy now myself – could do with a bit of kip. Oh well, off to bed – I'm handing over to Dr Wake who will monitor Arthur during the day.

Tuesday night – I nearly dropped off tonight but Dr Kant-Dropoff rudely shook me and shouted "Wakey-wakey" in my ear. I feel really cross with him.

Dr Kant-Dropoff writes. . .

Arthur seems more tired and irritable tonight. Shouted at me at 3 a.m. after I stopped him from falling asleep.

WEDNESDAY
Dr Wake writes. . .

Arthur is slurring his words today. He keeps repeating things and he moves about slowly. He can still play chess, though, and even beat me in a game. Obviously the areas of his brain dealing with thinking are still functioning normally.

Wednesday night – I'm not talking to Dr Kant-Dropoff after last night's row. Played loud music to keep awake. I could see Dr Kant-Dropoff didn't like it – ha-ha!

I'm really tired all the time now. If I close my eyes I could fall asleep. Got to keep going.

Dr Kant-Dropoff writes...

Arthur has been <u>extremely</u> quiet tonight.

Thursday

I don't like the way Dr Wake shouts "rise and shine" each morning. Why does she have to be so cheerful? I mean it's not as if I've been asleep. I bet she gets a good night's sleep, though...she must have something against me. Yes, that's it: *she's getting at me.*

Dr Wake writes...

Arthur is clearly exhausted and his pulse rate keeps going faster and then slower.

Thursday night - My beans on toast tasted funny tonight: I feel sure Dr Kant-Dropoff put some drug in my food. But why? WHY? Maybe he's getting back at me for playing loud music. I'll show him...

Dr Kant-Dropoff writes...

Arthur seems to be suffering from strange ideas. This is typical of people who lose too much sleep. We'll have to monitor the situation closely.

Friday – Refused to finish my cornflakes this morning – the milk tasted odd. Dr Wake gave them to me so she must be in on the plot with Dr Kant-Dropoff. Ha-ha! They think I don't suspect they tamper with my food.

4.15 p.m. When I stood up the floor was heaving like the sea. I must have been poisoned!

I'll be safe here. All quiet – I think Dr K-D's gone away. Phew, I can relax! Just close my eyes now for a minute... Zzzzzzzzzzz

Sunday evening - I've just woken up. I still feel really sleepy but all my tiredness has gone. The last few days seem like a nightmare. Did I really imagine the doctors were trying to poison me? And here they are now, all smiles with some tea and biscuits. They wouldn't harm a fly. That's the last time I miss a night's sleep. ...

CONCLUSION BY Dr Wake and Dr Kant-Dropoff

Arthur seems fully recovered. His pulse, heart-rate and brainwaves are normal. The experiment proves lack of sleep can cause mistaken thoughts and cause other problems such as disorders to the pulse and heartbeat. It appears these can be put right by a longer than usual period of sleep.

Bet you never knew!
Although scientists no longer keep people awake, in one experiment volunteers were woken up as soon as they started to dream. The scientists wanted to find out how the brain would act if it couldn't dream. The poor volunteers ended up getting woken over 30 times a night as their brains tried harder to make them dream.

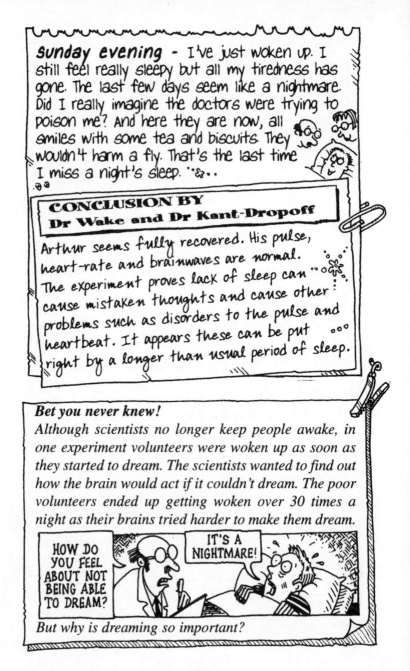

HOW DO YOU FEEL ABOUT NOT BEING ABLE TO DREAM?

IT'S A NIGHTMARE!

But why is dreaming so important?

Bulging fact file

NAME: Dreams

BASIC FACTS: Dreams are mixed-up memories that pass through your mind when you are asleep. Your cortex often puts them together to make a story.

DISGUSTING DETAILS: Scientists think that in the future a special kind of video camera could be invented to pick up signals in the neurons of your brain and turn them into pictures. So you could watch reruns of your happiest dreams and even your scariest nightmares – if you're brave enough.

SCIENCE CLASS DREAM

SICK SOUP DREAM

RAT PIE DREAM

SCHOOL DINNER DREAM

Let's imagine it's already possible: this is how it might happen...

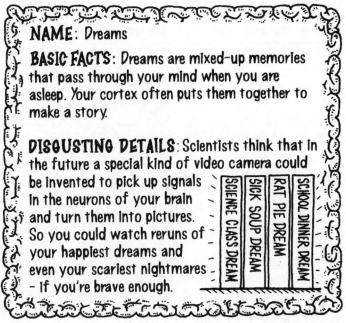

The Dream Machine

Congratulations on buying the NEW Dream Machine – the incredible machine that turns dreams into exciting videos.

PLEASE READ THESE INSTRUCTIONS CAREFULLY...

1 To set up the machine, plug it into your video. Strap the brainwave detecting hat to your head.

DREAM MACHINE

SLEEPY PERSON

VIDEO

BRAINWAVE DETECTING HAT

2 Go to sleep. Nothing will happen for at least 45 minutes as your body drifts from light to deeper sleep. As you relax your mouth might drop open and start to dribble – this is entirely normal.

3 After you have been to sleep for about 45 minutes your eyes will start moving under your eyelids. This is also perfectly normal. It is known as rapid eye movement (REM) sleep and it accompanies dreaming.

4 As you dream, your brainwaves will speed up and become irregular. This triggers the dream machine to start recording your dreams.

EEG PRINTOUT

5 You will not be able to move your body whilst dreaming. Your brain squirts a chemical into the brain stem that blocks nerve messages to your muscles. This is a sensible precaution to stop you sleepwalking.

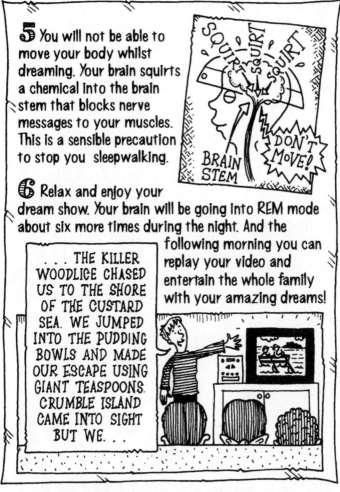

6 Relax and enjoy your dream show. Your brain will be going into REM mode about six more times during the night. And the following morning you can replay your video and entertain the whole family with your amazing dreams!

. . . THE KILLER WOODLICE CHASED US TO THE SHORE OF THE CUSTARD SEA. WE JUMPED INTO THE PUDDING BOWLS AND MADE OUR ESCAPE USING GIANT TEASPOONS. CRUMBLE ISLAND CAME INTO SIGHT BUT WE. . .

So what do you think of this invention? It sounds really good, doesn't it? Well, here's something else that will really get your little grey cells buzzing...

EPILGUE: SOMETHING TO THINK ABOUT

With its billions of neurons and synapses your bulging brain is the most complicated object in the known universe. So it's no wonder that people find it hard to get their heads round the science of the brain. Even the experts can't make up their minds.

Bishop Nemesius of Emesia (4th century AD) reckoned...

THINKING TAKES PLACE IN THE VENTRICLES

These are the fluid-filled spaces inside the brain, remember. One thousand years later Italian scientist Mondino de Luzzi (14th century) was convinced...

THE LINE OF FLESHY GORE IN THE VENTRICLES IS A WORM THAT CONTROLS THINKING

Yuck! He must have had worms on the brain.

And even modern-day scientists can have misleading ideas on the brain. For example, until the 1980s many scientists believed you could decode what the brain is thinking by looking at the pattern of neuron signals. But it's now known that this pattern varies according to your mood and your level of concentration (see page 113). This means that you can have exactly the same thought and yet each time produce a different pattern of neuron signals.

At present much of what we still don't know about the brain boils down to one awkward little word: why? Why do we have emotions? Why do we sleep?

Or, even over two hundred years after Franz Gall started wondering about it...

Question, questions, questions. What do you think?

Thanks to the brilliance of the human brain, people have walked on the moon and explored the depths of the oceans. But at present we still know more about the surface of the moon or the ocean floor than the workings of our own brains. No wonder some people think we'll never find out the whole truth about our brains. They would say...

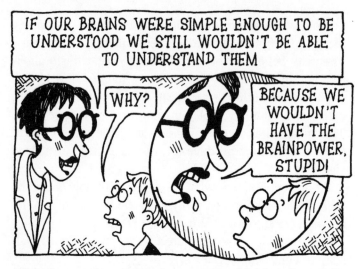

IF OUR BRAINS WERE SIMPLE ENOUGH TO BE UNDERSTOOD WE STILL WOULDN'T BE ABLE TO UNDERSTAND THEM

WHY?

BECAUSE WE WOULDN'T HAVE THE BRAINPOWER, STUPID!

(This does make sense – just you try thinking about it!)

But, on the other hand, it's the mystery that surrounds the brain that makes brain science so exciting. And although bulging brains in tanks or dream machines are still a few years off, scientists regularly make new discoveries. They might find a new brain chemical such as serotonin that affects mood. Or perhaps a new job for an area of the brain.

For example, in 1998 scientists at the University of Iowa carried out a remarkable experiment. Healthy volunteers and people with damaged amygdalas were shown photos of faces. The volunteers thought that some faces looked untrustworthy but the brain-damaged people couldn't make these judgements. The scientists believe that in addition to shaping feelings of fear and anger the amygdala makes us distrust others. (The amygdala is part of your limbic system – see page 37 if you don't remember.) So what do you think? Would you *trust* the scientists to get it right?

Well, one thing's for sure. Scientists will never cease to search for answers to the questions posed by the brain. And it's the ability to ask questions and to seek out answers that makes us human and our brains so unique.

That really *is* something to think about.

DISGUSTING DIGESTION

Introduction

Here's a disgusting science story…

It's ten minutes to the end of a particularly boring science lesson. The hands on the clock are crawling round like dozy snails. You're struggling to stay awake. It's so tedious.

BORED

BLAH, BLAH,
DIGESTION,
BLAH, TUBES,
BLAH, JUICES,
BLAH, BLAH

So you try to think about something – anything to stop yourself from dropping off. Lunch, perhaps? Yes, that sounds like a good idea. OK – so it's only school lunch but breakfast was centuries ago. You're so hungry. Couldn't you just murder a scrumptious steaming pudding oozing with hot jam and custard?

But then your teacher asks a tricky question.

What's the function of the Stomach?

Dead silence.

No one answers. Just then your tum lets rip with a huge, hearty rumble. It sounds deafening – just like a massive rumble of thunder. The echoes bounce off the classroom walls. Everyone stares at you. What do you do?

a) Turn scarlet and mumble "Sorry".

b) Blame the smart, goody-goody kid next to you.

c) Jump up, and close all the classroom windows saying, "There must be a storm coming, wasn't that thunder?"

A scientist, of course, would know the scientific answer. Some scientists actually spend their lives delving into digestion. Digestion is when food is taken into your body to help you stay alive and grow. It sounds about as thrilling as last night's dirty dishes.

But it doesn't have to be.

Digestion is disgusting. Amazingly disgusting! And this disgustingly amazing process is going on inside your body right now. In this book there are some foul scientific secrets and disgusting discoveries served up with a hearty helping of belly-laughs. And afterwards you'll be able to answer your teacher's question like this...

* (Bor-bor-rig-mus) Posh medical term for a rumbling tummy. The stomach walls squash the gas and liquids inside. The surrounding area wobbles too – making the sound louder.

After all, there are plenty of laws in science but not one of them says it's got to be boring. So now there's only one question. Have you got the stomach for some really disgusting discoveries?

Better read on and find out...

The young medical student turned white. His eyeballs bulged in his head and his mouth opened in a soundless scream. He wanted to yell but nothing came out. Not even a muffled gasp. He wanted to run. Run anywhere. But his legs wouldn't budge. He wanted to wake from his nightmare but this was no dream. It wasn't a scene from a horror film either. This was real life.

There really were sparrows flapping around the room. They were pecking at bits of dead body on the floor. And that really was a huge hungry rat skulking in the corner and gnawing greedily on a lump of human bone. This was a room in a hospital … and the year was 1821.

Don't panic! Hospitals aren't like this any more. But when 18-year-old medical student Hector Berlioz (1803-1869) visited a dissecting room in Paris this is what he really saw. (A dissecting room was where dead bodies were cut up so that their different parts could be studied.) This is just one example of the disgusting conditions endured by doctors and scientists in the past as they probed the secrets of digestion.

Disgusting digestion dates

The ancient Egyptians were into dissecting 5,000 years ago. In fact, every time they made a mummy they got their hands on the human guts. They always removed the intestines, or guts, and other vital organs and put them into jars because they would rot easily and spoil the preserved mummy. They kept all the body bits in jars for the mummy to use in the afterlife.

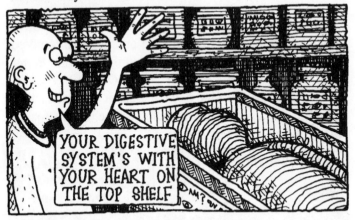

YOUR DIGESTIVE SYSTEM'S WITH YOUR HEART ON THE TOP SHELF

But the Egyptians weren't interested in the structure of the guts or how they worked. One of the first people to be genuinely interested in the guts was a foul-tempered Roman doctor.

Horrible Science Hall of Fame: Claudius Galen (AD129-201) Nationality: Roman

Galen said:

My father was amiable, just and benevolent, but my mother had a very bad temper. She used to bite the serving maids and was always shouting at my father.

Hope *your* mum isn't like that. Sadly Galen inherited his mum's temper and nothing much from his dad.

Young Galen was disgustingly clever. He wrote three books before he was thirteen and another five hundred after that. Some of them had intriguing titles like *Bones for Beginners*, *On the Black Bile*, and *On the Usefulness of Parts of the Body*. One day Galen kept 12 scribes busy as he strode up and down dictating the words for 12 different books at the same time.

DICTATE, BLAH BLAH, DRONE, WITTER

BIG-HEAD!

Galen reckoned he had the last word on medicine. He once said:

Whoever seeks fame needs only become familiar with all that I have achieved.

Modest, eh? The problem was Galen wasn't always right. In fact he was often WRONG. For example, he reckoned blood was made in the guts and went to the liver where it turned blue.

WRONG. Blood is made in the bone marrow and spleen. Just goes to show you can't believe everything you read in books. Galen said that humans only have 16 teeth. WRONG AGAIN – it's incredible that he never bothered to count them!

DO YOU MEAN I'M NOT NORMAL?

Galen made silly mistakes because he got his ideas from cutting up dead animals rather than humans. But no doctors dared to argue with him. They were scared of Galen's famously foul temper. (Once Galen had even dared to shout insults at an opponent in the sacred

Temple of Peace.) And they were even more scared he might ask his pal the Roman Emperor to dispose of them in a disgusting fashion.

For about 1,500 years doctors believed Galen's theories. They could have cut up a few bodies to check for themselves. But few did. Governments often banned dissection and where it *was* allowed doctors felt they were too grand for all the messy, gory cutting up stuff and left that to their humble assistants. Then a doctor came along who was...

A cut above the rest

Andreas Versalius (1514-1564) had a horrible habit. He stole dead bodies. And he wasn't particular either – anybody's body would do. Young, old, men or women – it didn't matter as long as the corpse wasn't too rotten. While he worked in the Belgian town of Louvain he used some disgustingly dodgy tricks to gain his revolting ends. He would:

• dig up bodies in cemeteries.

- steal the bodies of criminals left on public display.

- attend executions and sneak the body away at the end of the proceedings.

Then he would hide the bodies in his room. And late into the night by the flickering flame of a candle, he probed their grisly innards. Andreas Versalius wasn't crazy. He was a scientist and he was determined to go to any lengths to solve the mysteries of how the body worked. The appalling methods he used were the only way to get any answers. Dissection was banned, remember.

Things became easier in 1536 when Versalius became Professor of Anatomy in Padua, Italy. Here, the authorities were sympathetic to dissection. They even fixed execution dates so that the criminal's body would be nice and fresh for anatomy classes.

NOW I CAN'T MANAGE TUESDAY, WOULD WEDNESDAY BE O.K.?

You'll be pleased to know doctors no longer need to steal bodies to practise dissection. Some people actually agree to allow their bodies to be dissected after death to help train medical students.

Bet you never knew!
Here's how to play Andreas Versalius's favourite game.
1 Allow yourself to be blindfolded.
2 Ask your friends to hand you a selection of human bones.
3 Identify them by their shape and the way they feel.
4 You win if you get them all right.

ER, WELL, UM, I DON'T THINK IT'S A SKULL

Rotten reading

Versalius discovered more about the inside of the human body than anyone before him. He was the first person to describe the structure of the human guts accurately. In 1543 he published his discoveries in a book *The Fabric of the Human Body*. It was packed with tasteful pictures of bits of bodies and skeletons with lovely scenery to make the revolting subject matter nicer to look at. The book was a bestseller.

But Versalius came to a disgusting end. According to one story he was cutting up a nobleman's body when it twitched. The "corpse" was still alive! Versalius decided to make himself scarce and embarked on a long sea voyage. But poor old Versalius was shipwrecked and starved to death on a lonely island. And what's more he had no body to keep him company!

Could you have made these disgusting discoveries? Here's your chance to probe those gruesome innards and their grisly secrets. Delicate readers may find this next chapter not quite to their taste. It's a little bit sick.

Disgusting digestive bits 'n' pieces

Would you want to inspect the guts in grisly close-up detail? It's a horrible job but sometimes it's vital to check on problems. The scientist in this chapter has a real problem. He was absent-mindedly sucking his pen when he swallowed the top. It got stuck somewhere in his guts.

As luck would have it he'd just invented an incredible shrinking machine.

So all he needed was a volunteer to shrink down to 2.5 cm (1 inch) high and venture into his guts in search of the missing top. Any takers? Unfortunately, every doctor the scientist asked seemed to have an excuse. So he hired hard-bitten Private Eye, M.I. Gutzache for this unpleasant job.

First Gutzache had to change into special protective clothing so he wouldn't be digested during his hazardous mission.

Here's Gutzache's report. Go on take a look, you know you want to – it's fascinating.

Digestive bits and pieces

It seemed a cinch. Just a quick surveillance operation. "No problem," I said. So I took the job. That was my first big mistake. I may be a small-time private eye but under the shrinking ray I started to feel even smaller. But the worst was yet to come. I was going to be swallowed by a scientist!

Tough teeth

The teeth looked tough. There were several types. Some geared for biting, and some for chewing, gnawing or nibbling. They all looked mighty mean to me. Teeth are as hard as they come - d'you know you need a diamond to cut into them?

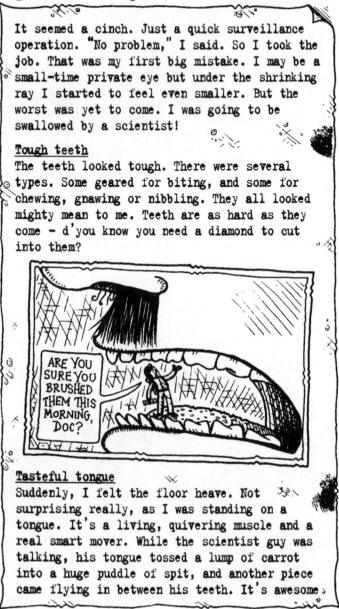

ARE YOU SURE YOU BRUSHED THEM THIS MORNING, DOC?

Tasteful tongue

Suddenly, I felt the floor heave. Not surprising really, as I was standing on a tongue. It's a living, quivering muscle and a real smart mover. While the scientist guy was talking, his tongue tossed a lump of carrot into a huge puddle of spit, and another piece came flying in between his teeth. It's awesome.

what that muscle can do! But if I didn't act
fast I figured I'd be next for a spit dunking.
I cast around for an exit.

Salivary (sal-i-very) glands
But I was too late, all of a sudden I felt
wet and hot. Looking down I saw I was up to
my knees in saliva (that's spit to you). It
looked like trouble - but trouble is my
business. I knew there were six hidden glands
pumping this stuff out. I was going to have
to swim for it. I dived down the gullet. It
seemed the safest place to be. But I was wrong.

The scientist writes …

I was trying hard not to bite Detective Gutzache.
It was actually quite lucky that he fell into my saliva -
it helped me to swallow him. Spit may seem disgusting
stuff, but it's full of proteins called enzymes that are
vital for digestion.

1. An enzyme joins on to another chemical in the food.

2. The enzyme splits up food molecules until they
are small enough to be sucked through my gut walls.
(There's a lot more of this going on inside my small
intestine!)

Then disaster struck. Gutzache got stuck in my gullet, or oesophagus (a-sof-fer-gus), to use the technical term. What would happen to him now?

Oesophagus

Just my luck to get wedged in his throat! The scientist guy started coughing and spluttering. My body shook as he gulped. Then I felt all this water flooding over me – I was on the move! Now, I often find myself in tight spots and I can tell you this next one was seriously tight. The sides of his gullet squeezed together forcing me down. Then I hit some half-chewed food. The gullet walls squeezed the food into a ball. I knew that I could be squashed too. I wanted out. But it was too late.

STOP SWALLOWING DOC!

The scientist adds …

My oesophagus walls squeezed together behind Mr Gutzache and pushed him down. This is called peristalsis (perry-stal-sis). It's Greek for "push around". It was lucky he didn't fall down my windpipe. That would have started me choking until I'd coughed him back into my mouth.

Stomach

I hit the stomach with a splash. It was more of a bellyflop than a dive. I found myself swimming in a lake of mush. It looked and smelled like sick. It was sick! I felt sick too. I was churned around as the stomach walls squeezed in and out. I felt like a sock in a washing machine. I figured the juice was acid because I could see it dissolving the food. I was real glad of my protective suit!

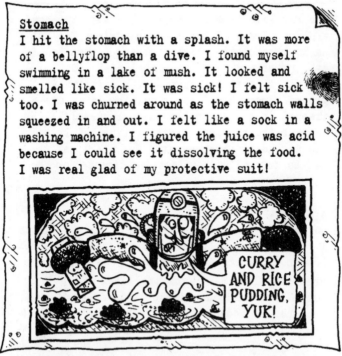

CURRY AND RICE PUDDING, YUK!

The scientist writes …

My stomach lining makes up to 2 litres (3.5 pints) of acid juice every day to dissolve the food I eat. And there are enzymes at work too.

Small intestine

After a few hours I managed to squeeze through the exit below the stomach. I found myself in a long tube that looked like a subway. I switched on my headlamp and peered at my waterproof map. My route was clear. I should head down the duodenum (dew-o-dee-num), jejunum (gee-june-num) and ileum (ill-ee-um). Whatever they were.

177

The map said "small intestine" – but it seemed endless. I knew I had to keep moving. The gut walls were closing behind me and I wasn't hanging around to get squashed again. So I walked. My feet squashed on the soft rubbery ground. Just then I saw something large and blue trapped in a fold in the wall. Success! It was the missing pen top. I gingerly pulled it out and tucked it under my arm. Now all I had to do was to get out without getting digested on the way.

A squirt

Suddenly I was splattered with digestive juices. I felt like an automobile in a car-wash, except I wasn't getting any cleaner. I was covered in brownish slimy bile from the liver and pale juice from the pancreas, I didn't stop to admire the view. I made tracks for the large intestine.

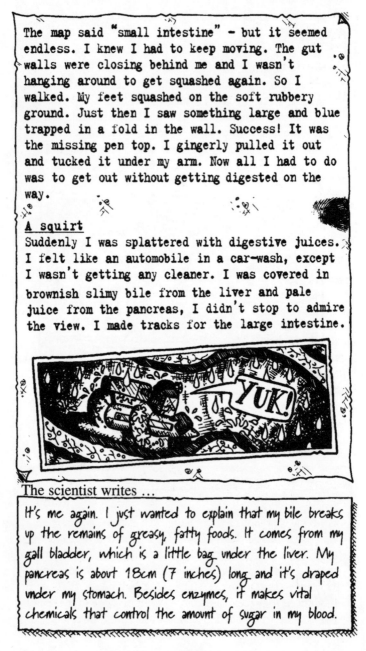

The scientist writes …

It's me again. I just wanted to explain that my bile breaks up the remains of greasy, fatty foods. It comes from my gall bladder, which is a little bag under the liver. My pancreas is about 18cm (7 inches) long and it's draped under my stomach. Besides enzymes, it makes vital chemicals that control the amount of sugar in my blood.

Appendix

In the large intestine I saw a weird sight. A little tube, about 5cm (2 in) long, leading to a dead end. In the end I figured it out. It was the appendix. It wasn't doing much – just hanging out, I guess.

The scientist writes …

Gutzache's got it right for once! My appendix spends its life doing nothing and I'm not even sure why it's there. My large intestine is definitely there for a reason though, it sucks up any spare water and minerals from my food.

The rectum

I was dead beat. So I sat down. Big mistake. I sank into something soft and brown and it didn't smell too good. I was in the rectum. It was the final stretch of the large intestine. And there was only one way out. I could see the toilet bowl. It seemed a long way down but there was nowhere else to go. I shoved the pen top out and it splashed into the water far below. *My turn next*, I thought.

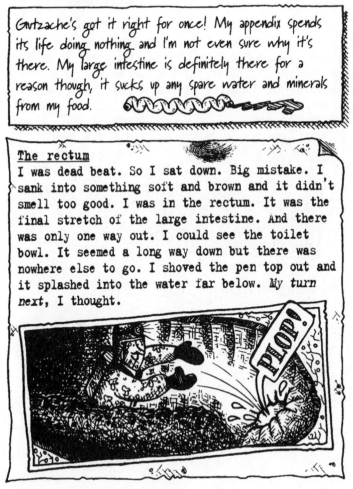

The scientist writes …

The large intestine is where waste food is stored.
Most of the spare water is sucked out of the waste
and through the sides of the gut. Er . . . 'scuse me a
minute. Got to dash . . .

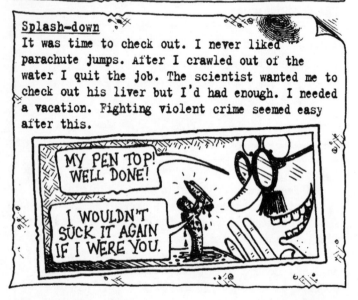

Splash-down
It was time to check out. I never liked
parachute jumps. After I crawled out of the
water I quit the job. The scientist wanted me to
check out his liver but I'd had enough. I needed
a vacation. Fighting violent crime seemed easy
after this.

MY PEN TOP!
WELL DONE!

I WOULDN'T
SUCK IT AGAIN
IF I WERE YOU.

Disgusting expressions

I SAW AN
INTERESTING
STOOL THIS
MORNING.

WAS IT IN A
FURNITURE SHOP?

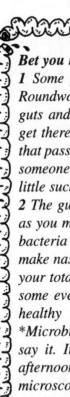

Bet you never knew!
1 Some people have worms in their guts. It's true!
Roundworms, pin worms and flukes can all live in the
guts and feast on half-digested food. They generally
get there in infected food. And once in, they lay eggs
that pass out of the body with the faeces ready to infect
someone else. But don't panic! Nowadays these nasty
little suckers can be beaten using drugs.
2 The gut also contains microbiological* bacteria or
as you might know them – germs. Up to 400 types of
bacteria happily swim around in the colon where they
make nasty smells. And they make up 1.5 kg (3 lbs) of
your total weight! But most of them are harmless and
some even make useful K and B vitamins to keep us
healthy (see pages 233-236 for more details).
*Microbiological means the study of tiny life. Go on,
say it. It's a brilliant word to chuck into a Friday
afternoon science lesson. It means you need a
microscope to see these bacteria because they're so
small. You could actually find hundreds on the pointy
end of a pin.

More bits'n'pieces

In his hurry to get away, Gutzache missed out a few important digestive bits and pieces. It's time to take a closer look at…

The life-saving liver

Tiny bits of digested food molecules in the blood go to the liver to make vital substances your body needs. The liver also does hundreds of other vital jobs such as making bile (see page 178).

The vagus (vay-gus) nerve

The vagus nerve is like a long telephone wire that "vaguely" snakes round the guts carrying messages to and from the brain. These include orders to squeeze the gut wall and move the food ball on to its next destination.

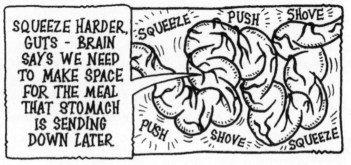

Crucial kidneys

These are the body's filters. As blood passes through them they clear out all the spare water and waste products and send them down for storage in the bladder.

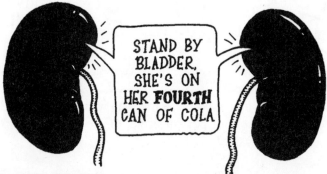

Bursting bladder

This is an incredibly wrinkled sack. It looks like a prune after a really long bath, but as it fills up, it gets bigger and it looks more like a balloon. The speed this happens depends on how much a person has had to drink. Most people need to pee about four to six times a day.

How can you tell when someone's bladder is full? Easy. They start twitching, writhing and dancing around looking for the nearest loo. If you were feeling heartless you could…

a) Join in the dancing.

b) Tell them not to worry – the bladder can store up to 400 ml (14 fl oz) of pee (or urine, to use the posh word for it) fairly easily.

In fact, the bladder is so strong that in an adult it can swell to 10 cm across without going pop.

Disgustingly odd bits'n'pieces quiz

Now you've checked out the main digestive bits, you've just got time to check out the obscure nooks and crannies. Doctors were probably having a laugh when they dreamt up some of the weird names for certain body bits. Can you guess which bits are inside you and which are made up?

1 Deaver's Windows
2 Islets of Langerhans
3 Crypt of Lieberkühn
4 The Pustule of Volvo
5 Flint's Arcade
6 Ferrein's Pyramid
7 Fibres of Mummery
8 Verheyen's Stars

Answers

1 TRUE. These are spaces in the flesh that hold the guts securely in position. The spaces are named after their discoverer, American scientist John Blair Deaver. **2 TRUE.** These are areas in the pancreas which make a hormone called insulin which controls the speed your body turns its food into energy. They're named after eagle-eyed German doctor Paul Langerhans who spotted them in 1869. **3 TRUE.** And what's more they aren't crypts where dead bodies are buried. They're tiny pits in the small intestine that produce digestive juices. But you'd be a dead body without them because they're vital to digest your food. **4 FALSE.** The Volvo is a Swedish car. **5 TRUE.** These are arch-shaped blood vessels in the kidneys and nothing to do with amusement arcades. They're named after their discoverer, American professor Austin Flint. **6 TRUE.** An area of the kidney above Flint's arcade. These pyramid-shaped bits were named after a French professor of surgery called Antoine Ferrein, who wrote about them in 1746. They're nothing to do with the pyramids in Egypt and you won't find a mummy skulking inside one. **7 TRUE.** These are stringy bits inside the teeth. They're nothing to do with mummies or pyramids either. **8 TRUE.** These are star-shaped veins on the kidney named after Philipe Verheyen who described them in 1699. Verheyen was planning to be a priest but he had an accident and doctors had to chop his leg off. He was so fascinated by this horrible ordeal that he gave up the priesthood. He decided to study medicine instead and became a professor.

185

Congratulations! You've finished the chapter. Feeling peckish? Desperate enough to eat a school dinner? Better scoff some now before you read about the vile food in the next chapter. It really takes the cake … or is it the biscuit?

I'M DESPERATE ... BUT NOT THAT DESPERATE

Foul food facts

This chapter is about food. It's about what we eat and how much we eat. But don't expect a mouth-watering feast. This is Horrible Science, remember, so you'll be reading about really foul foods. Got a brown paper bag handy? Good – you might need it!

THAT'S AMAZING! WE HAD SWEETCORN FOR DINNER, TOO!

Enormous eaters

In your lifetime you'll guzzle about 30 tonnes of food – that's the weight of six elephants or 20 rhinos. In one year the average greedy grown-up can munch their way through 78 kg (34 lbs) of potatoes, 26 kg (11.8 lbs) of sugar, 500 apples, 150 loaves of bread and 200 eggs, and still have room for pudding.

STOP MOANING BERNARD, WE ONLY GO SHOPPING ONCE A YEAR.

SUPERM

If you only ate boring pieces of bread and butter all the time you'd still get through about 250,000 slices in a lifetime. But some people eat a lot more than that.

All-time glutton Edward "Bozo" Miller of Oakland, California used to guzzle 11 times more food than anyone else. In 1963 he scoffed 28 chickens in a single stomach-splitting feast and became a legend in his own lunchtime. Now you might think that's a lot, but compared with some animals it's just a tiny snack.

• An elephant can knock back up to half a tonne of leaves and bark every day.

• Every day a blue whale swallows four tonnes of tiny sea creatures called plankton – that's more food than a human eats in a year. Mind you, the whale is 2,000 times heavier than a human.

• Even tiny creatures can munch more for their size than humans. For example, the 2 gram (0.07 oz) Etruscan shrew scoffs up to three times its own weight every day. That's like a human eating one entire sheep, 50 chickens, 60 family-sized loaves and 150 apples every day. You'd never cram all that into your lunch box, would you? So why do the shrews stuff their little faces? Well, they have to. Shrews need the energy all this food gives them to keep active and warm in cold weather.

Could you be a scientist?
If you like food, you don't have to become a chef. You could become a scientist instead. Yes, scientists have performed some mouth-watering experiments. Can you predict the results?

1 In the 1970s a group of American scientists went to a party and watched people eating. (Don't do this at parties – it's rude.) The scientists found that overweight people ate more than thinner people. The scientists quickly grabbed the food and took it into another room. What happened next?
a) The overweight people went into the next room to get the food.
b) The overweight people couldn't be bothered to move. The thinner people went next door and helped themselves.
c) A fight broke out and the scientists were chucked out for spoiling the party.

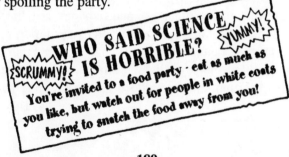

WHO SAID SCIENCE IS HORRIBLE? YUMMY! SCRUMMY! You're invited to a food party - eat as much as you like, but watch out for people in white coats trying to snatch the food away from you!

2 In the 1970s scientists at Virginia University, in America asked a group of people to sample a selection of yummy ice-creams after first slurping down a rich, sweet milk-shake. (And this was a science experiment?!) The aim was to see which group ate the most ice-cream.

What did they find?

a) People who were trying to lose weight ate more ice-cream.

b) People who were trying to lose weight ate less ice-cream.

c) Everyone scoffed as much as they could because the food was free and then threw up everywhere.

Enormous appetites

The amount you can eat depends on how big your stomach is. After all, you've got to put all that food somewhere. This is also controlled by a pea-sized lump on the underside of the brain called the hypothalamus (hi-po-thala-mus). This signals to your brain when it's time to eat and when to stop. If you don't want to stop, then chances are that you're eating something you really enjoy. And if you don't want to start eating, then you're probably sitting in front of your school dinner…

Foul food favourites

Food is vital. It does more than simply fill you up. It supplies the chemicals that your body needs to stay healthy and grow. But we all have foods we love. And we all have foods we love to hate. Here's a school dinner menu. Which dishes might tempt you?

~ School dinner menu ~

Thin soup (not sure what's in it, and it smells odd)

Greasy hamburger or tasteless vegeburger

Sickly stodgy pudding

Unspeakably greasy liver and onions

Chips that taste of cardboard

Rubbery cabbage

Watery yoghurt (you'll have to guess the flavour)

Bullet-hard peas

It's really strange, but some teachers and even a few otherwise quite normal people think school dinners are the height of good taste! Because that's all a favourite food is – just a matter of taste. Like most people you probably chose your favourite foods when you were about two years old. But all over the world people enjoy different foods. Including some that might seem horrible to you. We managed to talk fearless Private Eye M.I. Gutzache into sampling a few of these foreign delicacies.

Foul food report

It seemed like a good idea. No more swimming about in stomachs, no more parachute jumps. Just a lunch date. My kind of assignment, I thought. A private eye like me needs a strong stomach, so I reckoned I could face up to anything. I was wrong!

1 Haggis
(Scotland)

2 Chitterlings
(southern USA)

3 Frogs' legs
(China and France)

4 Prahoc
(Cambodia)

5 Sheep's eyeballs
(from a boiled head)
(Middle East)

<u>1.</u> Tasted good — I like the savoury taste of onions and herbs and meat. I was just enjoying my second helping when someone mentioned that the meat was sheep's heart and lungs wrapped up in its stomach. I suddenly needed some fresh air.

IT'S UPSET MY STOMACH

WELL HOW DO YOU THINK THE SHEEP FELT?

<u>2.</u> This was really good. Nice crunchy batter. Then they told me it was chopped pigs intestines with corn meal fried in lard. I swallowed hard and went on to the next dish.

IT KIND'A LEAVES A LUMP IN YOUR THROAT

NOW DON'T GO GETTING ALL EMOTIONAL ON US

<u>3.</u> I could see what this dish was. I shut my eyes and took a bite. It tasted like watery chicken. I'd prefer chicken any day.

VERY FRESH FROGS' LEGS, SIR. SAW THEM HOPPING IN THE POND THIS MORNING

4. Tasted a bit fishy. No, I don't mean fishy suspicious - just fishy and kind of salty. But when I learned the fish had been squashed to paste and left to rot for a few days, I decided they could keep their rotten fish.

IT'S ROTTEN FOOD

WELL, I WOULDN'T SAY THAT...

I WOULD - I WATCHED IT ROT!

5. I took one look at the eyeballs and they took one look at me. We were eyeball to eyeball. I started to sweat. I knew what I had to do, it was staring me right in the face. "OK, that's it," I snapped. "I quit!" This job was sick.

Poor old Gutzache, he couldn't cope with the eyeball because he wasn't used to eating that part of an animal. But if he eats tongue, breast and neck, what difference does an eyeball make? It's all a question of what you're used to. If Gutzache had grown up in the Middle East he'd have been eating eyeballs since he was two - and loving them!

And here's something else you shouldn't try.

Poison pills

Some people will eat just about anything. But would you believe that some people used to eat poison? In 1733 dangerously dodgy doctor Ned Ward sold antimony pills as a cure for everything including upset tummies. But antimony is a poison once used by the ancient Egyptians to bump off flies. So not surprisingly the pills caused

195

violent stomach pains. One joker wrote a poem about Ned Ward:

Before you take his drop or pill

Take leave of friends, and make a will.

But most people believed the adverts and thought the pain was part of the cure. The doctor made his fortune. He even gave poor sick people free samples of the wonderful pills. How kind! But oddly enough Ward never tried his own pills. This may explain why he lived to a ripe old age.

But antimony is just one of a host of disgusting poisons that turn up in food. Watch out, the next chapter could give you a nasty reaction…

TRIED ANY OF MY BRUSSELS SPROUT JAM YET, KIDS?

GAG!

RETCH!

Fatal food poisoning.

Food can be fatal. Well, not the food itself but what's lurking inside it. There may be all sorts of hidden poisons and germs lying in wait for your unsuspecting innards. So in order to protect yourself, you need to know all the disgusting details.

Disgusting poisons fact file

NAME: Poisons

THE BASIC FACTS: A poison is a chemical that gets into your body and makes you sick. Poisons include acids that dissolve the guts. Other poisons get to the brain in the bloodstream and knock the victim out.

THE HORRIBLE DETAILS: 1 Some of the deadliest poisons are called toxins. They're made by germs that get into food. Some can kill.

2 The best way for your body to get rid of a poison is to throw it back up again. That's why people spend the whole night throwing up after eating a dodgy dinner that's alive with germs.

Teacher's tea-break teaser

Try this teaser during a teacher's tea break. It'll be as welcome as a snail in a salad bar. Tap lightly on the staffroom door. When the door creaks open your teacher will be holding the regulation mug of sludgy mud-coloured coffee. Smile sweetly and say:

Answer

Coffee can be poisonous if you drink too much too fast. It contains a chemical called caffeine (also found in tea and cola drinks) that makes the heart beat faster. Normally it's quite harmless but scientists reckon that if someone drank 100 cups in four hours the caffeine would be strong enough to put their heart and blood vessels under fatal pressure.

Some good and some bad news

Here's the good news: it's not easy to get poisoned. As long as you're sensible about what you put in your mouth, you're not going to get poisoned by man-made chemicals. If it isn't a drink don't drink it, and if it isn't food don't eat it. And food poisoning caused by germs is fairly rare, too.

Now the bad news: crowds of germs hang around in the hope of causing some really foul food poisoning. At best these awful invaders cause an upset tummy. At worst they can kill – as you'll discover in the next chapter.

So what does food poisoning do to you? We've managed to get hold of a doctor's notes on a case of food poisoning. See if you can decipher the doctor's dodgy handwriting.

THE CASE OF THE POISON PORK PIE

The patient is in great distress. He's a teacher at Gunge Street School and says he ate an ancient pork pie in the school canteen. He now has pain in the intestines and is vomiting every half-hour and he's producing diarrhoea (runny faeces). I believe that the muscles of the patient's gut are squeezing all the food and water out of each end. The patient's body is trying to get rid of infected food. ...

DIAGNOSIS: The patient has food poisoning

TREATMENT: The patient needs complete rest from school for a few days. For the first day or two he should drink only flat lemonade or warm water with a pinch of sugar and salt. This should stop his body drying out or dehydrating, whilst the white blood cells from his blood move into the gut and eat up the remaining germs.

PROGNOSIS: He'll live to bite another day.

Yes, germs are always ready to attack us. As you'll find out on page 204, our favourite private eye M.I. Gutzache is hot on the trail of the germs. But the germs are hatching their own dastardly plans...

Germe top secret war plans

Right lads, our enemy is the entire human race. Your mission is to get into their food and drink and raid their guts. Your orders are to make 'em sick. Make 'em throw up, and make 'em really miserable. You will start your mission as soon as the fridge door opens. Read these plans carefully and then eat them. Good luck, lads!

TOP SECRET BATTLE PLANS~
KEEP OUT OF REACH OF HUMANS

1 GO UNDER COVER IMMEDIATELY

Good hiding places: soil, dirty water. Humans won't dare look for you there. Lumps of dung or rubbish bins provide even better cover.

SOIL   DIRTY WATER   DUNG   RUBBISH

2 GET MOBILE

Your first objective: get on a human's hands and fingers and clothes and then onto their food. Human fingernails provide excellent shelter, and they'll do the job for you. You'll be inside the body in no time!

A fly can offer first-class aerial support. Aim to be picked up from a cowpat when the fly drops in to suck up moisture. The fly will then proceed to rendezvous with human food. The fly sicks its digestive juices over the food and sucks up the mixture. Now's your chance to drop onto the food.

FLY   COWPAT   HUMAN FOOD

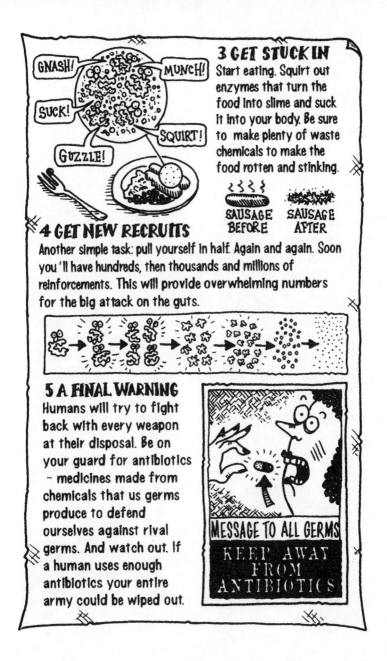

GNASH!

MUNCH!

SUCK!

SQUIRT!

GUZZLE!

3 GET STUCK IN

Start eating. Squirt out enzymes that turn the food into slime and suck it into your body. Be sure to make plenty of waste chemicals to make the food rotten and stinking.

SAUSAGE BEFORE

SAUSAGE AFTER

4 GET NEW RECRUITS

Another simple task: pull yourself in half. Again and again. Soon you'll have hundreds, then thousands and millions of reinforcements. This will provide overwhelming numbers for the big attack on the guts.

5 A FINAL WARNING

Humans will try to fight back with every weapon at their disposal. Be on your guard for antibiotics – medicines made from chemicals that us germs produce to defend ourselves against rival germs. And watch out. If a human uses enough antibiotics your entire army could be wiped out.

MESSAGE TO ALL GERMS

KEEP AWAY FROM ANTIBIOTICS

201

Dare you discover for yourself ... how things rot?

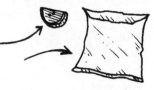

What you need
a piece of orange
a large polythene bag

What you do
Seal the orange in the bag and leave it in a warm place for six days.
What do you notice?

a) The orange stays the same.
b) The orange goes mushy and smelly.
c) The orange grows bigger.

How NOT to handle food
Here are some sure-fire ways to give germs a helping hand into your food...
• Sneezing into food.

• Coughing into food. This shoots germs from your mouth and nose into the air. Use a handkerchief. Do not wrap your food in the handkerchief or use it as a bandage afterwards. Germs can also get into your body through unwashed wounds.

• Handling food without washing your hands. (There are usually a few germs hanging around on your hands.)
• Picking your nose or biting nails. This is a marvellous way to pick up a few million germs. It's especially anti-social if you try to do both at the same time.

• Picking bits of food from your teeth with your fingers and then eating it. Not recommended.

Disgusting detective work

Following the sad case of the food-poisoned teacher (see page 199), we decided to investigate the school kitchen that was suspected of foul play and even fouler pork pies. It needed someone with experience, with dedication and above all … with guts. There was only one man for a case like this…

Another dirty job by M.I. Gutzache

FOUL FOOD REPORT by M.I. Gutzache

At last, some real detective work! Something undercover. I'd heard that school kitchens were clean places that were inspected regularly by public health officers. But this one was different. It proved a real dirty business. Stomach churning, in fact, but I got the pictures in the end.

Can you spot the germ danger signs in each picture?

Fresh food quiz

If cooks manage to get rid of bacteria they can keep food fresh for longer. Which of the following methods will work?

1 Boiling food and sealing it in an air-tight container.

2 Squashing the food and germs into a plastic box.

3 Mixing the food with lots of sugar or salt.

4 Smoking the food over a really smoky fire.

5 Sucking all the air out of the food so the bacteria can't breathe.

6 Freezing the food with the bacteria in it.

7 Drying the food out so the bacteria can't drink.

8 Spinning the food around really fast. The germs get so dizzy that they die.

Answers

1 Yes. Any thorough heating, as in cooking, will kill bacteria. Keeping food in an air-tight container such as the cans you buy in a supermarket will stop bacteria from getting back in. **2 No.** The bacteria will still live and breed, and destroy the food. **3 Yes.** The sugar draws water from the food and the bacteria can't live without water. That's why jam doesn't go rotten. **4 Yes.** The smoke covers the food with chemicals such as nitrites that kill the bacteria. This is what keeps smoked fish such as kippers fresh. **5 Yes.** This is what happens when food is vacuum packed. The food will keep in this form for months. **6 Yes.** The cold kills the bacteria. That's why food stays fresh in the freezer. **7 Yes.** The bacteria can survive as tiny seeds called spores, but drying out stops them from being active. **8 No.** Bacteria don't get dizzy.

We've painted a pretty grim picture of the germ world and maybe we're being a bit unfair. After all, they're just doing what comes naturally – for a germ that is. And we can't get rid of germs altogether. There are different germs in different countries and some will always manage to get into our bodies. Then our bodies have to fight against the disgusting, deadly digestive diseases that are lurking in the next chapter. BEWARE!

Deadly digestive diseases

If there's something even more disgusting than digestion then it's the dreadful digestive diseases that germs can cause. There's a long, horrible list of them and many are not just disgusting, they're deadly, too. We asked our Private Eye M.I. Gutzache to compile a dossier on the worst villains. Gunge Street School was in trouble. More teachers and some children too were going down with dangerous diseases. The kitchens needed inspection, there were various germs under suspicion. Gutzache was ready for the job.

A DEADLY GERM DOSSIER

by M.I. Gutzache

They're a real mean bunch of no-good low-lifes. Even I was shocked at the things these guys get up to. I shuddered to think they were hiding out in the very school kitchen I'd visited. These germs hit the young and the old hardest. That's bad news for young kids and tired old teachers. These germs must be stopped before they close down the school.

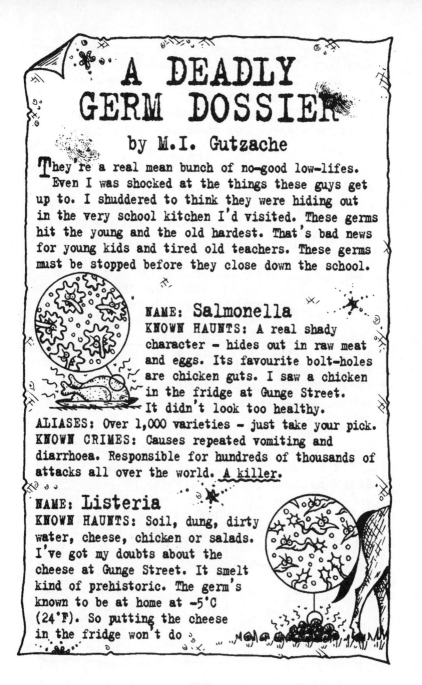

NAME: Salmonella
KNOWN HAUNTS: A real shady character – hides out in raw meat and eggs. Its favourite bolt-holes are chicken guts. I saw a chicken in the fridge at Gunge Street. It didn't look too healthy.
ALIASES: Over 1,000 varieties – just take your pick.
KNOWN CRIMES: Causes repeated vomiting and diarrhoea. Responsible for hundreds of thousands of attacks all over the world. <u>A killer.</u>

NAME: Listeria
KNOWN HAUNTS: Soil, dung, dirty water, cheese, chicken or salads. I've got my doubts about the cheese at Gunge Street. It smelt kind of prehistoric. The germ's known to be at home at -5°C (24°F). So putting the cheese in the fridge won't do

much good. This character is tough – it can even live at 42°C (106°F). If a human got that hot they'd need a doctor fast.
KNOWN CRIMES: Causes violent sickness. These germs could spoil your whole day.

NAME: Staphylococcus
KNOWN HAUNTS: Nostrils, on skin especially in cuts and boils. The Gunge Street cooks must have been crawling with these germs. The germs hang out on food that should be kept in the fridge but that's been left out too long. Like the awful smelling Gunge Street mince that was left out mouldering for three whole days.
MODE OF OPERATION: Gets on to food from un-bandaged cuts on hands.
KNOWN CRIMES: Causes diarrhoea, vomiting and painful cramps in the guts. These germs could spoil your whole week.

NAME: Clostridium botulinum
CAUSES: Botulism
KNOWN HAUNTS: Soil, fish, meat and vegetables.
MODE OF OPERATION: Thankfully no one's seen this germ at Gunge Street.
KNOWN CRIMES: Botulism causes double vision, weakness, difficulty talking and . . . DEATH.
WEAPONS: The toxin produced by this germ is deadly. Just 10mg (0.154 grains) could poison every human on Earth.

Conclusion

These guys are bad news. They must be rounded up. But it's going to be a tough job. They're a big mob and they've got so many hideouts. There's just one weapon that'll get them beat – and that's cleanliness!

But some germs are much more deadly and hopefully we'll never come across these criminal characters in Gunge Street kitchens ...

USEFUL WEAPONS

NAME: Vibrio cholerae
CAUSES: Cholera
KNOWN HAUNTS: Water mixed with faeces from another cholera sufferer.
MODE OF OPERATION: Gets into the body through eating shellfish that live in this dirty water. (Must be careful next time I eat oysters.) More usually spread by drinking the dirty water itself.

Drinking water sounded like a real dumb move. So I checked out the local water company and they said they had the problem sussed. They put chlorine in the water to blow the germs away.

KNOWN CRIMES: Causes violent vomiting, deadly diarrhoea and painful cramps. The victim's body dries out and turns blue. You could easily wake up to find yourself DEAD.

CHOLERA VICTIM

211

NAME: Salmonella typhi

KNOWN HAUNTS: The faeces of someone who has had the disease and survived. Typhoid is a relative of the notorious salmonella crime family — only these guys are even more vicious.

MODE OF OPERATION: Gets around on dust or flies or dirty fingers.

KNOWN CRIMES: Causes a rash and a nasty cough. Turns the victim's faeces into a green and runny soup. If untreated it kills 20 per cent of its victims. Hey, that's nasty!

NAME: Shigella dysenteriae

KNOWN HAUNTS: The guts and faeces, dirty water and food.

KNOWN ALIASES: Can be caused by amoeba — the scientist guy says that's a microscopic blob-like animal. I'll take his word for it. I just don't want to find this blob anywhere near my hot dog.

KNOWN CRIMES: Spreads from the guts to the liver and causes a deadly fever. It can even make holes in the gut.

Conclusion

I'm feeling sick. During my mission to the school kitchen I came over kind of hungry. Figured a piece of fruit wouldn't do any harm — now I've got pains in my gut and I'm feeling feverish. It's dysentry . . . I'm sure of it. ARGHH my guts! QUICK — where's the bathroom?

Over 1,000 years later one man was determined to stamp out the curse of dysentery and all the other deadly digestive diseases.

Horrible Science Hall of Fame:
Louis Pasteur (1822-1895) Nationality: French

Louis Pasteur had embarrassing table manners. He would fiddle with his bread. He'd tear a slice into crumbs and inspect them for dust and wool and bits of cockroaches. If he found anything suspicious he would examine it at the table using a portable microscope. (Don't start getting ideas now!)

WAITER! I ASKED FOR LEG OF LAMB, NOT LEG OF COCKROACH!

Next Pasteur would study the glasses. He'd wipe away tiny specks of dirt that no one else could see. And if that wasn't bad enough he'd launch into a loud and detailed account of his latest gruesome experiments with mice or bits of mashed up body and germs. This was because Louis Pasteur was obsessed with germs. He was so desperate to keep germs off his hands that he wouldn't shake hands with anyone. But oddly enough Mrs Pasteur didn't complain about her husband's habits. She was his most devoted helper.

Louis Pasteur was the deadliest enemy the germ world ever had. He hunted germs like a determined cop hunts a master criminal. With a total and ruthless dedication he worked weekends and evenings – refusing to give up ever. But then Pasteur had every reason to hate germs. Two of his children had died of typhoid.

At school no one thought young Louis was especially clever. His teachers said he was "passable" at Physics and "mediocre" at Chemistry. But Louis stuck at his science studies and eventually became a Professor of Chemistry. These are just a few of his achievements:

• He proved that germs make wine and beer go sour. This work involved going to vineyards and sampling wines (all in the interests of science, of course). Pasteur discovered that if you heat liquids to 72° C (161° F) for a few seconds you can kill germs without spoiling the taste. He had invented pasteurisation – which is used today to stop your milk going off too quickly.

• He went on holiday leaving a mix of chicken cholera germs and broth. (Chickens suffer a different type of cholera to humans.) When he got back he found that many of the germs had died. He gave the mixture of weakened germs to some chickens and found they stayed healthy. The chickens' bodies had produced chemical defences against the dead germs that they could use to fight living germs. We call the dead germs a vaccine and it's what you get when you're vaccinated against a disease.

COME ON, DON'T BE A CHICKEN . . . I MEAN DON'T BE SCARED

• Pasteur went on to develop vaccines against the killer diseases anthrax and rabies. The rabies vaccine was particularly welcome because rabies *always* kills its victims. Trouble is, the rabies vaccine had to be delivered by painful injections, but at least the victim gets to live.

Could you be a scientist?

In 1860 Pasteur climbed a mountain carrying sealed flasks containing yeast extract broth and sugar. At 1,500 metres (5,000 feet) he opened the flasks and filled them with cold mountain air then re-sealed them. Pasteur believed that the broth would only go off if germs from the air could get to it. He had already filled other flasks with air from the top of one hill, then another higher hill, and a cellar. What were the results?

a) All the flasks showed the same amount of germs. This proved that germs are found at all heights.

b) The most germs were found up the mountain and on the higher hill. This is because the wind blows germs up in the air.

c) The most germs were on the lower hill. The least germs were found up the mountain and in the cellar.

Answer
c) Pasteur proved that germs spread on specks of dust. The cellar was well sealed so the dust couldn't get in easily and the mountain air had even less dust so there were fewer germs. The germs couldn't get into the sealed flasks and their contents stayed fresh. In fact, one of the flasks from 1860 is now a museum exhibit and the broth is still fresh ... anyone want to try it?

Typhoid marches on...

Despite Pasteur's hard work he couldn't trace the deadly germ that had killed his children. The typhoid germ was eventually tracked down by Karl Joseph Eberth (1835-1926) in 1880. But the disease continued to claim lives. Edith Claypole (1870-1915), a talented American scientist, died of the disease in 1915. She was in the middle of a study of ... typhoid fever. And in 1909 doctors faced the killer disease again. Here are the facts in a story that tells how they might have happened.

Typhoid Mary

New York, 1909

Mary Mallon was a killer and her lethal weapon was ice-cream. Delicious, home-made ice-cream. But could it really kill people? Guns or bombs, maybe – but ice-cream?

And Mary didn't look dangerous. She was a shy woman of about 40 years of age with grey hair tied neatly in a bun. She wore small round spectacles and her plump figure seemed an excellent advertisement for her wholesome cooking. No wonder Dr George Soper felt confused as he stood in the kitchen in Park Avenue.

Surely Mary wouldn't harm a fly?

Then the doctor noticed Mary's hands. Big red raw hands that were used to hard kitchen work – hands that hadn't been washed in a week. They weren't just dirty – they were filthy. Every hollow and vein and knuckle was smeared with grime, and there was thick, black dirt under her fingernails.

"Well, sir, why did you want to see me?" she asked in her soft Irish voice. "I haven't got all day. The people here are taken badly. The daughter is dead and the servants are sick. I've lots to do."

The doctor pulled himself together. He had difficult and unpleasant things to say. "Mary Mallon, I have reason to believe you are spreading an infectious and fatal disease."

Mary didn't even blink. It was as if the doctor had said something about the weather.

"I don't know what you're talking about, sir," she said quietly.

"Let me explain," said the doctor. "Last year you worked as a cook at Oyster Bay, Long Island. Six people in that house fell sick with typhoid fever."

"So they got sick. People do – what's that to me?" asked Mary sounding a bit more annoyed.

"I talked to the family and I checked what they ate. The family all said they enjoyed eating ice-cream. Your ice-cream that you always make by hand."

Mary's mouth drooped crossly at the corners and she slowly pulled open a drawer under the table.

"You've had eight jobs in seven years," continued the doctor grimly. "And in seven of those eight houses there have been cases of typhoid fever."

Mary's filthy fingers groped for the meat cleaver.

"Mary," said the doctor coldly, "I think the typhoid was spread on your dirty hands."

"ARRRGGGGH!" With a banshee wail Mary threw herself on the doctor. She screamed in fury, "I'll learn ye. You meddling doctor – I'll chop ye up for sausages. I'll have ye for breakfast. I'LL KILL YE!"

Dr Soper leapt sideways just in time. The heavy cleaver hacked into the table top. He tore round the kitchen chased by Mary brandishing her weapon.

Dr Soper escaped and gasped out his story to New

York's Chief of Police. The police moved in swiftly. They raided Mary's house and found her hiding in an outside toilet. It took seven policemen to carry her shrieking and wailing to a waiting ambulance.

A few months later at the Riverside Hospital for Communicable Diseases in New York, Dr Soper sat in his office a little uneasily. The time had come for a talk with Mary. Or "Typhoid Mary" as the newspapers were now calling her.

"Typhoid is a terrible disease," began the doctor. "You get fever, spots, stomach pains, a cough and bowel movements that look like pea soup. But you'll remember all that, won't you Mary?"

"Why should I remember anything?" asked Mary grumpily. She glared up at Dr Soper's two hefty assistants who stood either side of her. Ready for the first sign of trouble.

Dr Soper sighed, "Our tests prove that you've had the disease. Although you got better, the germs are still in your gall bladder. They pass out of your body every time you visit the toilet. Some germs get on your hands and if you don't wash them they also get onto food."

"I don't understand," moaned Mary, "I'm a cook. I do

me job but no one tells me nothing."

Then Dr Soper offered his reluctant patient a choice. She could give up cooking or she could stay locked up in the island hospital. For ever.

"You can't keep me here," protested Mary. "Why are you doing this to me?"

Dr Soper grimly shook his head. "Oh, but we can keep you here, Mary. We have the legal power. But you do have another choice. Allow us to cut out your gall-bladder. It's a risky operation, but you'll be free of germs after we've done it. And then we'll let you go."

"I'll kill ye!" spat Mary struggling with the two assistants. "I'll never let ye near me gall-bladder – whatever that is."

But three years later Mary had a change of heart. Not about the operation, though. She agreed to give up cooking and report to Dr Soper every three months. But after she left the hospital she promptly disappeared.

In 1915 an epidemic of typhoid fever hit New York's Sloane Hospital for Women. Two members of staff died. One morning the kitchen maid was having a laugh with a friend. "That old cook, Mrs Brown," she sniggered, "she's so grumpy and guess what? She looks just like that woman in the papers a few years ago. What's-her-name – Typhoid Mary!"

Listening at the door, the cook, who was really Mary Mallon, clenched her dirty fists in rage.

Once again Mary disappeared but this time the police were on her trail. She was arrested soon afterwards. Mary Mallon had knowingly spread typhoid and people had died. How do you think she was punished?

a) Mary Mallon was executed for murder. The judge said: "Mary, you are too dangerous to live."

b) Mary was drugged by Dr Soper and while she was unconscious he removed her gall bladder. When she was completely free of typhoid germs the doctors let her go.

c) She was locked up on the island for the rest of her life.

Answer

c) Mary spent the rest of her life in prison. She was the first known carrier of typhoid fever and although she was never charged with a crime she was judged a menace to public health. In 1923 the doctors built her a cottage in the hospital grounds and gave her a job working in the hospital lab that studied germs – such as typhoid.

Today Mary Mallon is world famous as "Typhoid Mary." All she ever wanted to do was to make ice-cream. But her name is linked for ever to a disease she never truly understood.

The fight goes on

Louis Pasteur's work showed scientists how to discover germs and how to develop new drugs and vaccines to combat them. Today doctors cure typhoid using drugs. Meanwhile, the world-wide battle against other diseases continues. For example, in the 1970s 4,000,000 children a year were dying of cholera. In 1974 World Health Organization scientists invented a drink made from clean water, minerals and sugar which can be given to cholera victims to stop them drying out. This simple drink, named ORT (oral re-hydration therapy), has saved the lives of thousands of children.

So that's the answer. If we can keep germs at bay we can all live happily ever after. Er, no. Here comes the really bad news. Eating clean food can make you ill! Some people even die from their diets! Will you be able to stomach the next chapter? Better read on and find out...

A horribly healthy diet

There's a lot more to food than meets the eye. There are loads of vital ingredients that you must have in your daily diet. To find out more we persuaded Private Eye M.I. Gutzache to sneak back into the school kitchens to collect samples. At first he said he couldn't face going back to that revolting place. But after a bit of bribery and gentle persuasion with a roll of banknotes he dragged himself off his sick bed.

Gutzache goes into … school dinners

It was time for the protective suit. And I insisted on a gas mask for this dirty job. Some of the samples smelled kind of ancient. They were days old, and I figured they could be emetic. (Hey, I'm starting to talk like a scientist! An emetic is something that makes you sick as a dog.)

Sample 1 – A school potato
This rather sad potato was about to be boiled in a school dinner. But it was still a healthy specimen. This is what I found hiding inside it:

Slug*
81 per cent water
0.4 per cent protein
16 per cent carbohydrates
(in the form of a
chemical called starch)
0.1 per cent fat
0.8 per cent fibre
0.7 per cent vitamins
1 per cent minerals

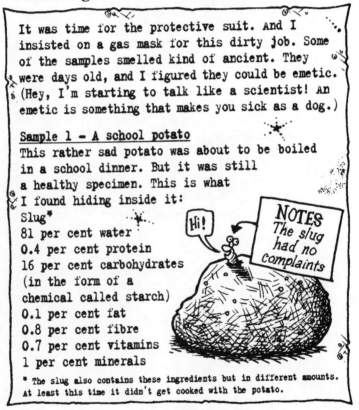

Hi!

NOTES
The slug
had no
complaints

* The slug also contains these ingredients but in different amounts. At least this time it didn't get cooked with the potato.

Sample 2 - A glass of water

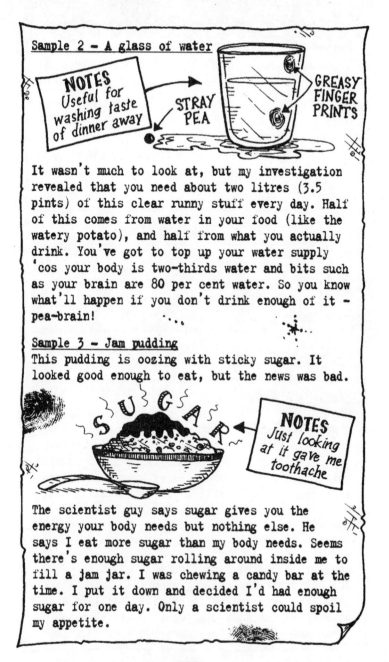

NOTES
Useful for washing taste of dinner away

STRAY PEA

GREASY FINGER PRINTS

It wasn't much to look at, but my investigation revealed that you need about two litres (3.5 pints) of this clear runny stuff every day. Half of this comes from water in your food (like the watery potato), and half from what you actually drink. You've got to top up your water supply 'cos your body is two-thirds water and bits such as your brain are 80 per cent water. So you know what'll happen if you don't drink enough of it - pea-brain!

Sample 3 - Jam pudding

This pudding is oozing with sticky sugar. It looked good enough to eat, but the news was bad.

SUGAR

NOTES
Just looking at it gave me toothache

The scientist guy says sugar gives you the energy your body needs but nothing else. He says I eat more sugar than my body needs. Seems there's enough sugar rolling around inside me to fill a jam jar. I was chewing a candy bar at the time. I put it down and decided I'd had enough sugar for one day. Only a scientist could spoil my appetite.

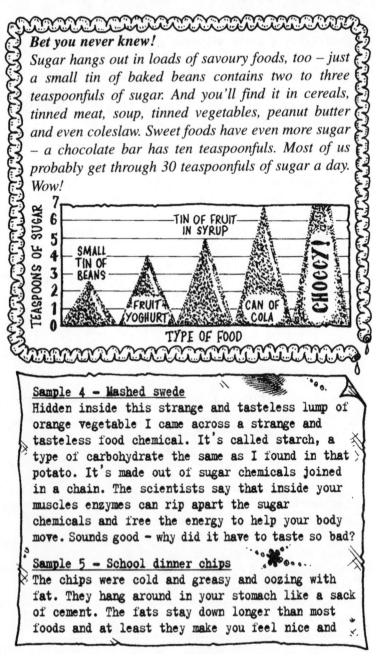

Bet you never knew!

Sugar hangs out in loads of savoury foods, too – just a small tin of baked beans contains two to three teaspoonfuls of sugar. And you'll find it in cereals, tinned meat, soup, tinned vegetables, peanut butter and even coleslaw. Sweet foods have even more sugar – a chocolate bar has ten teaspoonfuls. Most of us probably get through 30 teaspoonfuls of sugar a day. Wow!

TEASPOONS OF SUGAR

7
6
5
4
3
2
1
0

SMALL TIN OF BEANS

FRUIT YOGHURT

TIN OF FRUIT IN SYRUP

CAN OF COLA

CHOCCY!

TYPE OF FOOD

Sample 4 – Mashed swede

Hidden inside this strange and tasteless lump of orange vegetable I came across a strange and tasteless food chemical. It's called starch, a type of carbohydrate the same as I found in that potato. It's made out of sugar chemicals joined in a chain. The scientists say that inside your muscles enzymes can rip apart the sugar chemicals and free the energy to help your body move. Sounds good – why did it have to taste so bad?

Sample 5 – School dinner chips

The chips were cold and greasy and oozing with fat. They hang around in your stomach like a sack of cement. The fats stay down longer than most foods and at least they make you feel nice and full. But it seems spare fat turns into body fat slopping lazily around your stomach and backside. And get this - there's usually enough fat in your body at any one time to make seven bars of soap!

NOTES
Created oilslick disaster in my stomach

Sample 6 - School prunes

Hmm, prunes. Can't say I liked the taste, they had a weird kind of leathery texture. But my investigation showed that's 'cos they're loaded with fibre. That's the stuff that makes brown bread chewy and fruit and veg stringy. Seems your body can't digest fibre but it keeps the rest of your food moving in the gut. The gut walls can grip the fibre more easily than ordinary food. In the end this gets moving, too ... to the bathroom.

Sample 7 - Smelly cheese

NOTES
Relieved to find the smell wasn't from my socks

GHASTLY PONG

Some of the kids I interviewed had strange ideas about where the cheese came from. Well, I wasn't here to find out about its past - I was looking for the inside story and I found it. Cheese is

25 per cent protein – your body uses this substance to build muscles. Although your body is 20 per cent protein you don't need tonnes of the stuff. If you're 12 years old you need about 55 grams (2 oz) of protein a day. That's as much as a grown man, even though you're smaller. You need more protein because you're growing. Protein also hangs out in milk, cheese, fish, meat, beans and nuts.

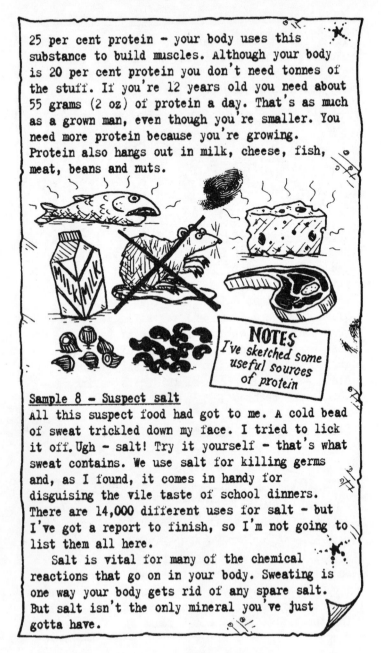

NOTES
I've sketched some useful sources of protein

Sample 8 – Suspect salt

All this suspect food had got to me. A cold bead of sweat trickled down my face. I tried to lick it off. Ugh – salt! Try it yourself – that's what sweat contains. We use salt for killing germs and, as I found, it comes in handy for disguising the vile taste of school dinners. There are 14,000 different uses for salt – but I've got a report to finish, so I'm not going to list them all here.

Salt is vital for many of the chemical reactions that go on in your body. Sweating is one way your body gets rid of any spare salt. But salt isn't the only mineral you've just gotta have.

Mysterious minerals

The school dinner samples were loaded with mysterious minerals. They're vital in tiny amounts for building your body and making useful chemicals.

You might be amazed to learn that your school dinner contains all these strange and foul-smelling chemicals. Oh – you aren't? Well, your teacher might be…

Test your teacher

Try testing your teacher or even your school cook (if you dare) on this fascinating topic.

1 Sulphur is a foul-tasting chemical but it makes up 0.25 per cent of your body. How much sulphur is that?
a) Enough to kill all the fleas on a dog.
b) Enough to kill all the fleas on an elephant.
c) Enough to kill all the fleas on a rat.

2 Iron is a vital mineral that your body uses to give blood it's brilliant red colour. What happens when you don't eat enough?
a) Your blood turns yellow.
b) You come out in spots and a fever.
c) You become pale and tired and don't feel like eating.

3 Your body is 0.004 per cent iron (lucky it doesn't rust!). How much iron is that?

a) Enough to make the head of a pin.

b) Enough to make a 5 cm (2 inch) nail.

c) Enough to make an iron lump the size of your arm bone.

4 Calcium is a vital raw material for bones. A 12-year-old child needs 700 mg (0.02 oz) of calcium a day. What's that equal to?

a) Four plates of spinach.

b) 40 plates of spinach. (Yuk!)

c) No spinach because this vegetable doesn't contain calcium.

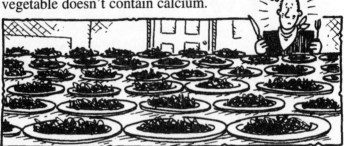

PLEASE LET IT BE c)

5 What's the best source of iodine?

a) Rainwater

b) Snails

c) Seaweed

IT'S a) AND c), NOT b), DEFINITELY NOT b)!

Answers

1 a) That is if your dog has fleas, of course! Warning: don't eat too much sulphur or it won't just be the fleas that get bumped off. **2 c)** The red bit in blood is a chemical that takes vital oxygen around your body. Lack of iron causes anaemia (a-nee-me-a). If you don't eat anything the anaemia gets worse. **3 b)** But that's no excuse to start sucking rusty old nails. No – it's much easier to get your iron from liver, wholemeal bread, dried fruit or treacle. **4 a)** You'll find the same amount of calcium in three glasses of milk, 16 large slices of bread or 85 g (3 oz) of cheese. Take your pick. **5 c)** Iodine is the most amazing mineral of the lot. Read on to find out why…

Getting it in the neck

You only need 0.004 grams (0.00015 oz) of iodine every day. But without it life is a pain in the neck. Here's why.

Iodine comes from the sea – that's why seaweed has so much of it. The iodine gets blown inshore as sea spray and collects on plants.

You eat them. A special part of your neck called the thyroid gland uses the iodine to make a chemical called thyroxine (thi-rox-een). Thyroxine makes your body grow and use up food faster.

IS YOUR THYROID GLAND SWOLLEN?

NO, I'M CHOKING ON A PING PONG BALL, YOU TWIT!

Without enough iodine the thyroid gland swells up as it tries to filter every last drop of the mineral from your blood. It forms a hideous lump called a goitre (goy-ter).

In the 1800s part of the mid-west USA furthest from the sea was known as the "goitre belt". There was less iodine there so, of course, more people developed goitres.

You'll find lots of iodine in seafood, fish and, of course, seaweed (if you can face eating it).

Could you be a scientist?
This disgusting experiment is common in university science courses. The aim is to show how thyroxine works. Take one harmless little bull-frog tadpole. It can take up to two years to turn into a frog. Feed it one drop of thyroxine. What happens next?
a) The tadpole turns into a frog.
b) The tadpole turns into a giant tadpole.
c) The tadpole grows a goitre.

Answer
a) Within a few hours the thyroxine turns the tadpole into a tiny frog the size of your little fingernail. Sadly, when the other tadpoles become frogs they're 100 times bigger. And given half a chance they'll gobble up their tiny brother or sister.

Vital vitamins
Vitamins aren't an optional extra. They're vital chemicals that keep you healthy. They're so important that you can buy lots of different pills and drinks that aim to provide extra vitamins. The adverts are everywhere:

Vit A

Carrot-cocktail-Slurp

Do you suffer from spots? Having trouble shaking off the dandruff? Can't see in the dark? You could be missing out on vitamin A. Vit A Carrot-Cocktail-Slurp is the obvious answer.

Just one slurp and you'll be spotting black cats in coal cellars! Yes that lovely vitamin A makes a chemical called visual purple at the back of the eye, so helping your eyes to see better in poor light.

BEFORE

AFTER

THE SMALL PRINT
You CAN get too much of a good thing. Drink too much Vit A Vita-Slurp and your hair will fall out and you could die. Yes DIE. Too much vitamin A can poison you which is why people can die if they eat a vitamin A-rich polar-bear liver.

Ingredients: extract of liver, milk, butter, eggs, fish and carrots.*

*That's why people say that carrots help you see in the dark.

233

Vit B

Get-up-and-go-Slurp

Tired and run-down? You need Vit B Get-up-and-go-Slurp! Why not try all ten mouth-watering varieties?

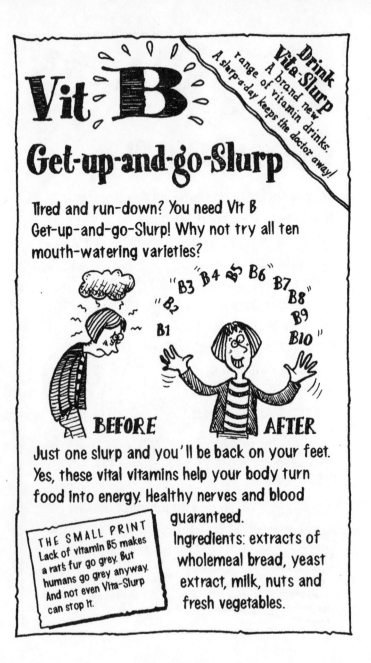

"B3 "B4 B5 B6 "B7 B8" B9 B10" "B2 B1

BEFORE   **AFTER**

Just one slurp and you'll be back on your feet. Yes, these vital vitamins help your body turn food into energy. Healthy nerves and blood guaranteed.

THE SMALL PRINT
Lack of vitamin B5 makes a rats fur go grey. But humans go grey anyway. And not even Vita-Slurp can stop it.

Ingredients: extracts of wholemeal bread, yeast extract, milk, nuts and fresh vegetables.

234

Vit D Sunny-Slurp

▶ Do your fingernails break at awkward moments?

▶ Are you getting enough vitamin D a day?

▶ One slurp of Vit D Sunny-Slurp and you'll be D-LIGHTED!

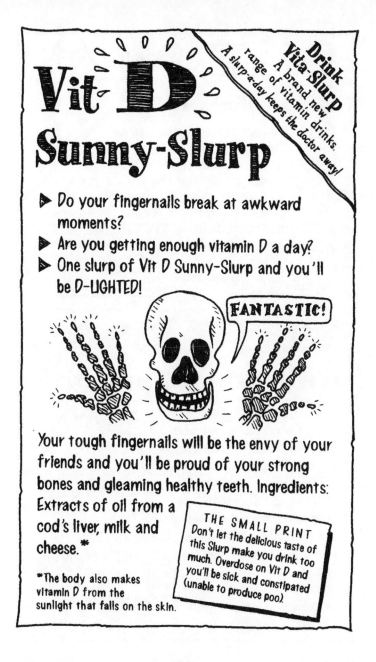

FANTASTIC!

Your tough fingernails will be the envy of your friends and you'll be proud of your strong bones and gleaming healthy teeth. Ingredients: Extracts of oil from a cod's liver, milk and cheese.*

THE SMALL PRINT
Don't let the delicious taste of this Slurp make you drink too much. Overdose on Vit D and you'll be sick and constipated (unable to produce poo).

*The body also makes vitamin D from the sunlight that falls on the skin.

Vit ~E~ Suppleskin-Slurp

Do you have tired sagging skin? Are there strange brown marks, or liver spots, on your hands? You need a shot of Vit E Suppleskin-Slurp. In no time you'll be glowing with good health and all those nasty cuts and bruises will be healing up fine. And you'll have a healthy blood system, too! Ingredients: extracts of wholemeal bread, butter and brown rice.

BEFORE

AFTER!

THE SMALL PRINT
Some people have baths in Vit E Suppleskin-Slurp in a bid to stay young-looking. But this is going too far - it doesn't work - sorry!

Drink Vita-Slurp A brand new range of vitamin drinks. A slurp-a-day keeps the doctor away!

Vit ~K~ Kwik-clot Slurp

Are you having trouble with clots? (No, not stupid people – we mean *blood* clots.) When you cut yourself, do you just keep bleeding? Essential for those more serious wounds, Vit K Kwik-clot Slurp will help your blood to clot-a-lot, so it stays where it belongs – that's inside your body, and not all over the carpet!
Ingredients: extracts of green vegetables and liver, and germs from the human gut!

IT'S SO ANNOYING!

BUT NOT ANY MORE

Drink Vita-Slurp A brand new range of vitamin drinks. A slurp-a-day keeps the doctor away!

OK – got the message? Missing out on vitamins makes you sick. But it took doctors many years to discover which foods were the best sources of which vitamins. Here's the story of one man's search for the truth about the most horrible sickness of all – scurvy.

The terror of the sea

Stinking bad breath, swollen purple gums, easy bruising, wounds not healing, bleeding eyeballs, tiredness and death. Yep. Scurvy was no picnic. A few hundred years ago you could walk round any port and spot the sickly seafarers a mile off. They were the ones with no teeth.

But why did sailors suffer from scurvy more than other people? For sailors in the 18th and early 19th centuries it wasn't just the sea that was rough, life on board ship was pretty rough, too. Conditions were really grim and scurvy used to be the terror of the sea. Sailors feared catching scurvy more than shipwrecks, pirates or shark attacks. But for years no one knew what caused this terrible disease.

But some captains thought they knew…

And, of course, the captains had their favourite cures…

Ship's doctor James Lind (1716-1794) felt sure these cures were useless. But he had to prove it. He reckoned that the disgusting food on board ship was part of the problem. In the days before fridges and freezers it was impossible to keep food fresh at sea. So a typical meal looked like this.

1 HARD TACK AND MAGGOTS.*

2 WATER THAT STANK LIKE A BLOCKED TOILET.

3 STALE CHEESE WITH MORE MAGGOTS.

4 SALTY BACON.**

5 GREASY RANCID BUTTER

*A dried biscuit so hard that a London museum has a 200 year example. You had to tap your hard tack before you ate it to get the maggots out.

**It was so salty that it made you thirsty enough to drink the disgusting water.

But which of these foul foods caused scurvy? Or maybe as the food was so horrible, the seafarers were missing out on something in their diet. Perhaps they were getting the disease because of something they *weren't* eating. Here's how James Lind might have written up his research:

Here's how James Lind might have written up his research:

HMS Salisbury, somewhere in the English Channel, 1747.

It's so frustrating. Here I am with 12 sailors sick with scurvy. I'm sure they're missing something in their diet - but what? I can't watch them die - I'm the doctor, I've got to try something. I'll have to experiment. I've always wanted to be a scientist. I'll divide the sailors into pairs and get each pair to try a cure suggested by other doctors. One of them has to work! Here goes!!

Sailors Walker Planke and Spike de Gunn will get a few drops of sulphuric acid a day. (Note: Mustn't make it too strong or it'll dissolve their guts.)

I'll give Davy Jones-Locker and Andy Cutlass two spoonfuls of vinegar a day.

I'll give Wilby Sicke and Len Ho a cup of seawater a day.

Jim Ladd and Roger Jolly will eat garlic and horseradish bound together with smelly plant glue.

W.P.
S.d.G.
D.J.L.
A.C.
W.S.
L.H.
J.L.
R.J.

240

Chivers Metimbers and Downey Hatch
will get a daily quart of cider.
Our two stowaway female crew
members Eve Too and Raisa Anchor
will each get two oranges and
a lemon a day.

Fourteen days later

Eve and Raisa are cured! I'm brilliant! (Shame
about the others, though.) The girls leapt out of
their hammocks on the sixth day and raced each
other round the ship. They said they hated all
that nasty sour fruit but felt much better
anyway. They've offered to
help me nurse the other ten
who are still sick.

1 Poor
Walker and
Spike are in a bad way. I feel
a bit sorry for them. They've
still got scurvy and now they've
got raging gut ache, too. Must
be all that acid.

2 Davy and Andy are in
a sour mood. That'll be the
vinegar. And they've still
got scurvy.

241

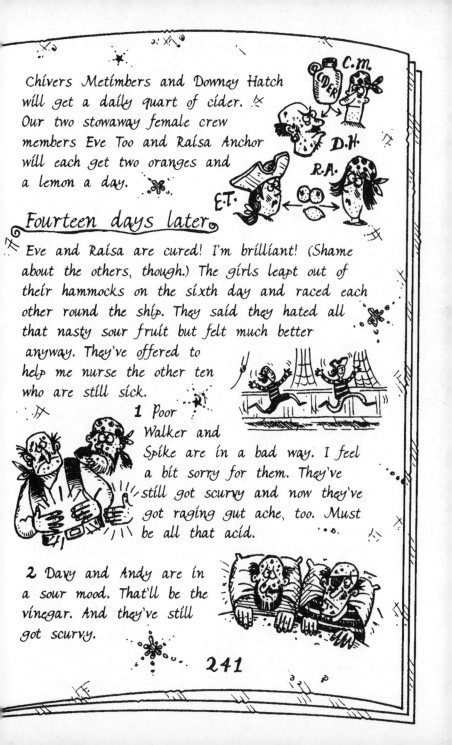

3 Poor Wilby and Len keep throwing up. Must be all that seawater. They've still got the scurvy.

4 Everyone steers clear of Jim and Roger. They reek of garlic and they can't stop farting. Ah, now that'll be all the horseradish. No improvement in the scurvy.

5 Chivers and Downey have still got scurvy, but at least they're happy. They keep singing "Roll out the barrel!" and shouting "Cheers!" to all the others. The rest of the crew have all volunteered to try this treatment.

Conclusion
I've cracked it - with a bit of help from these brave long-suffering seafarers! I'm really certain that scurvy can be cured by eating fresh fruit. Yes - that's the answer. I'm sure you get the disease if you miss out on some chemical in these foods.
IT'S FANTASTIC - I can't wait to tell everyone!

James Lind sent his report to Admiral Lord Anson (1697-1762) who was in charge of the Royal Navy. He thought Anson would support him. After all when Anson sailed round the world in 1740-1744 most of his crew had died of scurvy. So what happened next?

a) Lord Anson was impressed. Lind was given a £20,000 reward and in future all seafarers were ordered to eat a lemon a day. No one got scurvy ever again.

b) The Navy ignored Lind's findings and it took another 40 years before they took action.

c) The Navy decided that the acid treatment was better. Lind was sacked from his job as a nuisance and a trouble-maker.

Answer

b) Disgusting but true. The Navy decided that lemons were too expensive. They actually felt it was cheaper to hire new sailors to replace the ones who died. Things only changed after the sailors mutinied and demanded lemons to beat scurvy. Although some sailors didn't like the fruit they changed their minds when lemons and limes were added to their rum ration. But it wasn't until the 1930s that scientists found the mystery chemical that prevented scurvy was ascorbic acid – better known as vitamin C.

A disgusting diet

So, eat lots of different foods and you'll get everything your body needs to stay healthy. Brilliant! But what happens if you are vegetarian and don't eat meat or fish? Or if you're vegan and don't eat meat, fish or foods made by animals such as milk and eggs? Either way it's fine as long as you get the vitamins and minerals you need.

But eat just a few things and you won't get all the vital goodies. The most disgusting diet of all is not to eat anything. Surprise! Food is good for you, hunger is bad for you. Scientists have found that children who miss breakfast find it hard to learn new things at school. Don't try this excuse. And just look what happens to a really starving body...

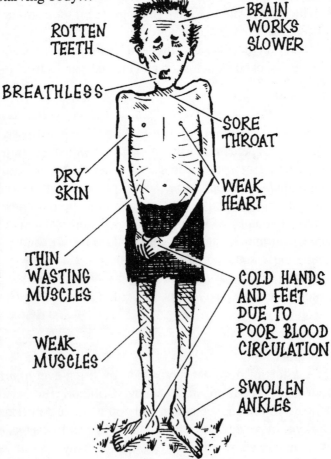

ROTTEN TEETH

BRAIN WORKS SLOWER

BREATHLESS

SORE THROAT

DRY SKIN

WEAK HEART

THIN WASTING MUSCLES

COLD HANDS AND FEET DUE TO POOR BLOOD CIRCULATION

WEAK MUSCLES

SWOLLEN ANKLES

Miserable, isn't it? In the bad old days hunger was a cheap way of punishing naughty children.

Luckily, you're equipped with the perfect gear to chomp any kind of food. The next chapter will really give you something to chew over.

The mighty mouth

Shovel food in your gob and something disgusting happens. Your food, even the stringiest steak and crunchiest carrots, turn into a shredded gooey pulp before vanishing for ever down the black hole of your throat. So what's going on? Get your teeth into these amazing facts.

Dare you discover for yourself ... what's in your mouth?

Stand in front of mirror. Open wide. Go on – take a look – it won't bite you. What do you see? An amazing chewing machine – that's what.

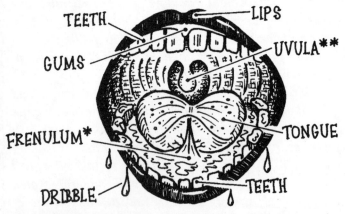

TEETH   LIPS

GUMS   UVULA**

FRENULUM*   TONGUE

DRIBBLE   TEETH

*This supplies your tongue with blood. Can you see the blood vessels? Pretty, aren't they? Well, pretty disgusting really.

**This little dangling bit hangs around in the throat and no one knows quite what it's for. It seems to help you swallow and its name means "little grape" in Latin – can you see why?

The talented tongue

The tongue is a lump of muscle. You can take a good look at it in the mirror, it's one part of your digestive system you can actually see, but don't go showing it to headteachers, parents, etc. Your talented tongue is amazingly agile. It moves around while you eat, talk or even eat and talk at the same time.

Disgusting taste fact file

NAME: Taste

THE BASIC FACTS: Your tongue is covered in tiny bumps called papillae (pap-pill-ay). Can you see them? On their sides are even tinier clumps called taste buds. Your brilliant buds pick up tastes and send the info. along nerves straight to your brain.

TONGUE TASTE AREAS

SOUR   BITTER   SOUR   SALT   SWEET

I FEEL SICK AND DIZZY – IS IT THE MONOSODIUM GLUTAMATE IN THIS MEAL?

EITHER THAT OR THE SLUGS

THE HORRIBLE DETAILS: There's a chemical called monosodium glutamate (mon-o-so-di-um gloo-ta-mate) that boosts your sense of taste. It's found in some Chinese recipes. But it makes some people feel sick and dizzy.

Some tasteless facts

1 According to the Chinese there are only three main tastes. Hot and fiery = spicy curry; onion/garlic = when you don't want to make any new friends; delicious = the fresh vegetables you have with your main course.

2 Western scientists disagree. They say that you can taste four tastes – sweet, sour, salty and bitter.

3 But your tongue can recognize hundreds of flavours made up of a mixture of tastes. Take crisps, for example. There are over 70 flavours including chocolate, strawberry, and hedgehog*. (It's true – manufacturers really did make crisps in these foul flavours.)

ER, WEASEL AND ONION. OR IS IT TOAD AND VINEGAR?

* Before you get on the phone to the World Wide Fund for Nature, they don't use any dead hedgehogs – this is an entirely man-made flavour.

4 Some people have sensitive taste buds. Cheese experts can sample a really smelly cheese and tell exactly where the cheese was made, whether the milk that made it was heated, and even what time the cow was milked. But if they're wrong they can get a bit cheesed off.

5 A doctor always looks at your tongue to check your state of health. For example, a thick white scum on your tongue might be caused by a disgusting infection called thrush (nothing to do with tweety-birds that eat worms).

6 In ancient China doctors peered at tongues too. They

believed that the appearance of the tongue reflected the health of the rest of the body. Here are a few things they looked for...

a) Whitish tongue = lack of energy.

b) Bright red tongue = body is too hot.

c) Purple/blue tongue or purple spots = blood not moving fast enough.

d) Fur-like growth* on the tongue = death will follow within a week.

*This could really be a sign the body is unwell. The "fur" may be a type of fungus which flourishes when the body's defences, the white blood cells, are weakened by other diseases.

Here are two experiments that are in the best possible taste.

Dare YOU discover for yourself 1... Test your taste

What you need
2 small cubes of uncooked potato
2 small cubes of apple

All you do is
1 Close your eyes and hold your nose. Ask someone to hand you one of the foods.

2 Put the food in your mouth and try to guess what you're eating. Now try the other food.

3 Stop holding your nose and repeat step 2. What do you notice?

a) It's easier to make out tastes when you hold your nose.

b) It's harder to make out tastes when you hold your nose.

c) Foods taste sweeter when you hold your nose.

Dare YOU discover for yourself 2...
Can you change your sense of taste?

What you need
Your favourite wine gums or fruit flavoured sweets. (Tell your parents you need them for science homework – if they believe that, you might as well go for extra pocket money while you're at it.)

2 extra extra strong mints or an ice-cube. Put it in a glass of water for a few seconds first.

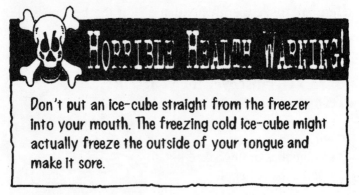

Don't put an ice-cube straight from the freezer into your mouth. The freezing cold ice-cube might actually freeze the outside of your tongue and make it sore.

All you do is
1 Pop the extra strong mints OR the ice-cube in your mouth. Keep it there until it melts.

2 Pop the wine gum in your mouth. What do you notice?

a) You can't taste it easily.

b) It tastes twice as fruity.

c) When you take it out of your mouth it's gone black.

Disgusting teeth fact file

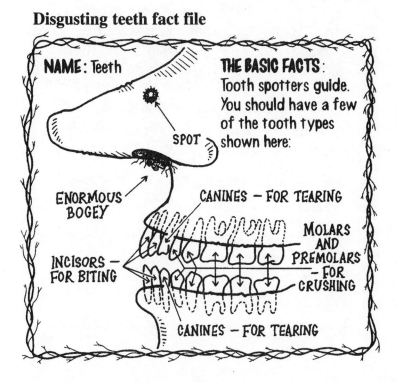

NAME: Teeth

THE BASIC FACTS: Tooth spotters guide. You should have a few of the tooth types shown here:

SPOT

ENORMOUS BOGEY

CANINES – FOR TEARING

INCISORS – FOR BITING

MOLARS AND PREMOLARS – FOR CRUSHING

CANINES – FOR TEARING

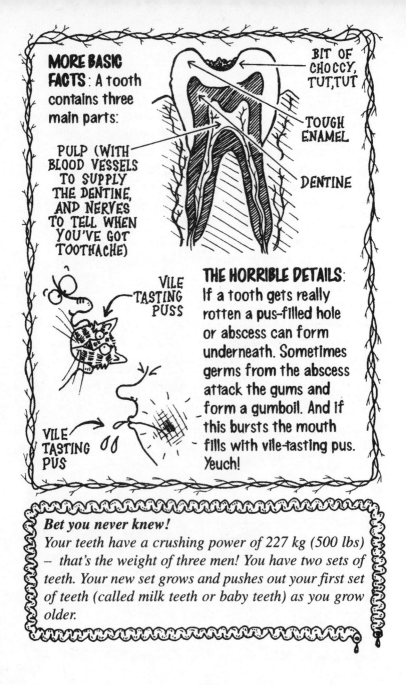

MORE BASIC FACTS: A tooth contains three main parts:

BIT OF CHOCCY, TUT, TUT

TOUGH ENAMEL

DENTINE

PULP (WITH BLOOD VESSELS TO SUPPLY THE DENTINE, AND NERVES TO TELL WHEN YOU'VE GOT TOOTHACHE)

VILE TASTING PUSS

VILE TASTING PUS

THE HORRIBLE DETAILS: If a tooth gets really rotten a pus-filled hole or abscess can form underneath. Sometimes germs from the abscess attack the gums and form a gumboil. And if this bursts the mouth fills with vile-tasting pus. Yeuch!

Bet you never knew!
Your teeth have a crushing power of 227 kg (500 lbs) – that's the weight of three men! You have two sets of teeth. Your new set grows and pushes out your first set of teeth (called milk teeth or baby teeth) as you grow older.

But that's nothing…

• Elephants have only four teeth but they are replaced six times. When the last set of teeth falls out the elephant starves.

POOR OLD THING! IT'LL BE PORRIDGE FROM NOW ON

• Crocodiles grow new teeth whenever they need them. This could be handy for humans, too. You could grow extra teeth to handle all those rubbery school dinners.

I'VE GROWN MINE TO HANDLE RUBBERY SCHOOL CHILDREN

• Sharks have 12 rows of teeth and if they lose a few, more will grow in their place.

B-B-BUT YOU MIGHT LOSE SOME TEETH IF YOU BITE INTO MY RUBBER SUIT…

SO WHAT?

Dreadful dentures

Humans only get two sets of teeth and when these fall out we're stuck. That's why millions of people have to wear false teeth or dentures. Nowadays these are made from a tough plastic but before then people had to make do with some really disgusting dentures. Here are a few examples…

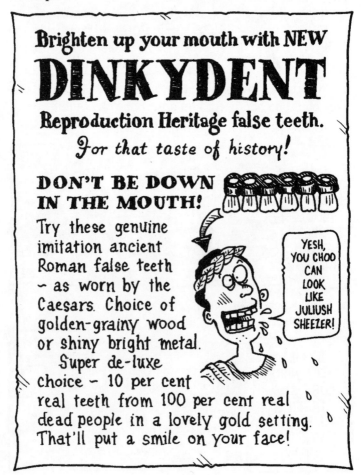

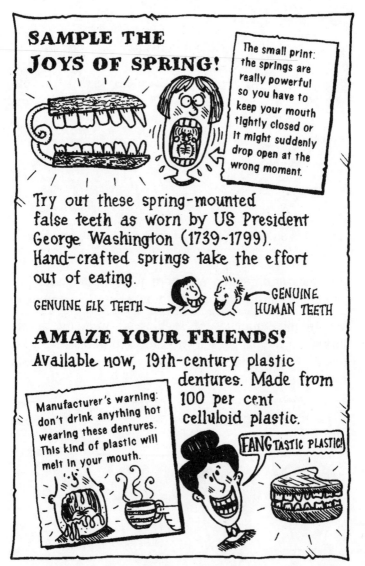

SAMPLE THE JOYS OF SPRING!

The small print: the springs are really powerful so you have to keep your mouth tightly closed or it might suddenly drop open at the wrong moment.

Try out these spring-mounted false teeth as worn by US President George Washington (1739~1799). Hand-crafted springs take the effort out of eating.

GENUINE ELK TEETH — GENUINE HUMAN TEETH

AMAZE YOUR FRIENDS!

Available now, 19th-century plastic dentures. Made from 100 per cent celluloid plastic.

Manufacturer's warning: don't drink anything hot wearing these dentures. This kind of plastic will melt in your mouth.

FANG TASTIC PLASTIC!

Of course, you'd probably rather not have false teeth. So it's a good idea to take care of the ones you've got.

Disgusting expressions

Isn't this an ornamental sign found in public buildings?

Answer: No, this kind of plaque is a disgusting layer of germs and bits of food that builds up around the teeth.

Within three minutes of sucking a sweet the germs lurking in the plaque start making acid to dissolve your teeth. If they make a hole they can cause horrible toothache.

Here are some disgusting ideas to help for making a clean sweep of the problem.

256

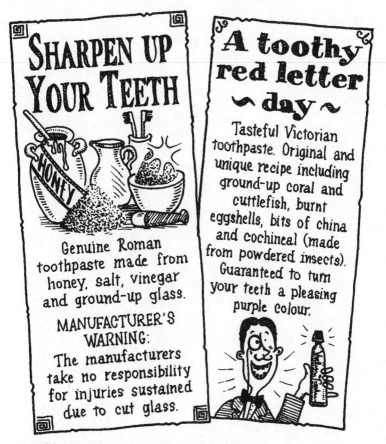

SHARPEN UP YOUR TEETH

Genuine Roman toothpaste made from honey, salt, vinegar and ground-up glass.

MANUFACTURER'S WARNING:
The manufacturers take no responsibility for injuries sustained due to cut glass.

A toothy red letter ~ day ~

Tasteful Victorian toothpaste. Original and unique recipe including ground-up coral and cuttlefish, burnt eggshells, bits of china and cochineal (made from powdered insects). Guaranteed to turn your teeth a pleasing purple colour.

And here are some more sensible ideas.
• Flossing teeth cleans out germs lurking between teeth and near gums – some of their favourite hiding places.
• Chewing a sugar-free chewing gum makes you produce spit. Spit contains chemicals that help combat the acid made by tooth germs, and so helps to keep your teeth clean.
But don't do either of these in science lessons. Instead, you could try this…

Teacher's tooth test

Does your teacher know the tooth – er, sorry, the truth about teeth? Find out now as you ask…

1 How many teeth does a child of ten have?

a) About 52

b) About 12

c) About 26

2 Which of the following isn't a raw material of modern toothpastes?

a) Chalk

b) Seaweed

c) Washing-up liquid

Super-slurping spit

Picture your favourite food. A giant pizza with your favourite topping and hot bubbling cheese. Sizzling juicy burgers or crispy fried chicken and a giant pile of fries. Can't you smell that lovely just-cooked aroma? Are you drooling yet? You should be. Just thinking about food makes your mouth water – and the smell and sight of food helps even more. Your spit is ready and waiting to come out whenever you need it.

Spit is made by six salivary glands – two under your tongue, two under your jaw and two under your ears. When you get mumps the salivary glands under your ear get infected by a virus and swell up so your face looks fat. But cheer up face-ache – help is at hand...

Ye Olde Mumps Cure

1 Take a donkey's lead and put it around the patient's neck.

2 Lead them three times round a pig sty.

After that embarrassing experience you probably wouldn't care about having a swollen face. Every day your sensational salivary glands squirt out 1-1.5 litres (1.8-2.6 pints) of spit. All of this you swallow. Some people spit it out instead – disgusting! Don't do it. It's a waste of good spit – look what it can do for you.

Have you ever eaten really dry food, like bread, when your mouth is also dry and there's nothing to drink? Disgusting, isn't it? By making your food wet, spit makes it easier to swallow. And spit helps you taste food. You can only taste food by detecting chemicals floating around in water. When food is dry its chemicals can't flow amongst the taste-buds so it seems tasteless.

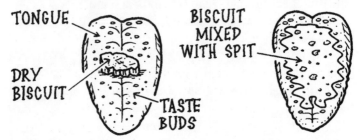

TONGUE

DRY BISCUIT

TASTE BUDS

BISCUIT MIXED WITH SPIT

Spit has some disgusting ingredients, such as mucus – basically the same stuff that streams from your nose when you have a cold. This makes it quite slimy and stringy so you can suck it back into your mouth. There's no need to demonstrate this interesting scientific accomplishment just now.

I SAID, THERE'S NO NEED TO DEMONSTRATE THIS INTERESTING SCIENTIFIC ACCOMPLISHMENT JUST NOW!!

Then there are the germs. Your spit is swarming with them. In fact, there may be 100,000,000 (one hundred million) bacteria in your mouth at any one time. Many germs end up getting eaten when you swallow spit. Hmm, tasty! But strangely enough, spit contains chemicals that kill some germs, and dentists have found that spit helps to keep your mouth clean and free from infection.

Spit also contains a waste product called urea that your body makes from spare protein. And guess what? You'll find it in urine too – it gives urine its yellow colour. If you eat too much protein your body makes more urea and your spit also turns yellow. Either that or you've been slurping extra thick banana milkshakes. But the real magic spit ingredient is an enzyme called amylase (am-me-laze) that rips carbohydrates apart into the sugars that make them up. (You can find out more about enzymes on page 283.)

Disgusting eating habits
Mealtimes used to be tough for kids.

261

One of the worst things to do when you're eating is to eat too quickly. Like these people...

Fast food facts

- Do you like pickled onions? If you find them disgusting you'll be horrified to hear that Pat Donahue crunched 91 in 68 seconds in Victoria, Canada in 1978.

• Peter Dowdeswell ate 144 prunes in 31.27 seconds in Rochester, New York, in 1986. Prunes are full of fibre and are well known for making you want to go to the toilet. So you can guess what the next world record was…

AH YES, CERTAINLY SIR. YOU'LL FIND THEM OVER BY THE...

• In the same year Peter also ate 91.44 metres (100 yards) of spaghetti in 12 seconds in Halesowen, Britain. And then … well you can guess what happened next.

BURP

Disgusting digestion expressions

GLASS OF LEMONADE?

NO, THANK YOU, IT CAUSES ERUCTATION

Is this dangerous?

Bigger, better burps

Huge hearty great burps are just your body's way of getting rid of some of the air you swallowed with your food. The faster you eat and the more you talk as you eat the more you burp. It's easier to burp when you're standing up. So imagine a posh party where people are eating and talking, and drinking fizzy drinks (with lots of gas) and standing up, too. They all want to burp but they're far too polite.

By the way, if you ever go to lunch in Arabia it's OK to burp loudly after the meal. It's considered a sign of good manners. This is sensible because you've got to let the air out somehow.

CONGRATULATIONS! You've managed to eat your supper without hiccups, heartburn, burping or food dribbling out of your nostrils. NOW for the tricky bit. Can you keep it down?

The Staggering Stomach

You're in control. You decide what you eat, don't you? Think again. There's a part of your body that seems to have a mind of its own. It's a muscular bag just under the left part of your chest. It makes you feel sick, it makes you feel queasy and it rumbles. And it does a whole load of other tricks, too … it's staggering!

Disgusting stomach fact file

NAME: Stomach

THE BASIC FACTS: The stomach is a storage tank for your food. Its job is to mix and squash food to make it easier to digest. The stomach also makes enzymes that digest protein and milk. And it does all this while you get on with your life.

THE HORRIBLE DETAILS: The stomach is staggeringly horrible. For example, there's a type of germ that lives quite happily in the stomach eating up your half-digested food.

GOOD OLD STOMACH!

RUMBLE CHURN, GURGLE, PLOP!

Staggering stomach statistics

The human stomach can hold up to 4 litres (7 pints) of food.

Mind you, that's nothing.

• It takes your speedy stomach just 60 minutes to digest a cup of tea and a jam sandwich.

- Milk, eggs and meat take a bit longer. Eat a boiled egg with a ham sandwich washed down with a milkshake and it'll take 3-4 hours to clear the stomach.
- But if you really want your stomach to work harder try a huge three-course dinner with soup and meat, and fruit for afters. That'll take your tired-out tum 6-7 hours to process.

- A wolf's stomach can hold 4.5 litres (8 pints) of food. Does that mean they have to "wolf" their meals?
- Cow stomachs can hold 182 litres (40 gallons) of food – that's enough to fill a bath if the cow sicked it up again. (Cows have an advantage – they actually have four stomachs not one.) One stomach is used for storing the grass before they sick it up and re-chew it – lovely! This is known as "chewing the cud" – or rumination (roo-min-ay-shun) as the scientists call it. The other stomachs are useful for storing the re-chewed grass whilst it rots. (Rotten grass is easier to digest.) Yum-yum!

• The mangrove monkey eats leaves all day. It needs an extra big tum to hold all those leaves and its stomach weighs as much as the rest of its body. If you had a stomach this big you really would be staggering.

Staggering stomach quiz

How well do you know your own stomach?

1 The word stomach comes from the Greek word for "throat". TRUE/FALSE

2 Butterflies in your stomach aren't anything to do with the stomach. TRUE/FALSE

I'VE GOT BUTTERFLIES IN MY STOMACH

IT'S PROBABLY THOSE CATERPILLARS I PUT IN YOUR SANDWICHES

3 It's possible to live without a stomach. TRUE/FALSE

4 It's possible to eat and eat until your stomach bursts. TRUE/FALSE

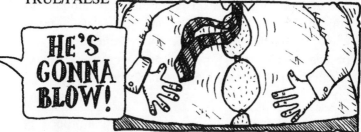

HE'S GONNA BLOW!

5 When you eat ice-cream the cold freezes your stomach. TRUE/FALSE

6 Your stomach stops moving when you're asleep. TRUE/FALSE

7 Your stomach produces an acid strong enough to dissolve a lump of bone. TRUE/FALSE

The vital goings on in the stomach were first probed by a scientist with a taste for staggeringly sick experiments.

Horrible Science Hall of Fame: Lazzaro Spallanzani (1729-1799) Nationality: Italian

Brainy Laz wanted to be a lawyer until his even brainier cousin Laura Bassi (1711-1778) talked him into becoming a scientist. As luck would have it, Laura happened to be the world's first woman professor of physics and introduced Laz to her scientist pals. So Laz became interested in many areas of science including such scintillating topics as where thunder clouds and sponges come from. (That's the sea creatures, not the cake you eat for tea or the thing you use in the bath.)

Laz had a hands-on approach to science. When locals claimed that Lake Ventasso in Italy had a giant whirlpool, the brave scientist built a raft and sailed across the lake – so proving the whirlpool didn't exist. In 1788 he decided to study volcanoes so he climbed a series of Italian craters. At Mount Etna in Sicily he had to be rescued after getting knocked out by poisonous gases. Undaunted he climbed Mount Vulcano but gave up when his walking stick caught fire and his feet got burnt.

Finally, by watching Mount Stromboli he discovered that gas explosions are the reason rocks fly out of volcanoes.

It took more than a few disgusting sights to stop Laz in his tracks. In 1765 he became interested in how some animals can re-grow parts of their bodies. So he cut up thousands of unfortunate worms, slugs and salamanders.

(He discovered that younger animals are best at re-growing.) He took the same fearless approach to his work on digestion. Would you want to make yourself sick? Laz did – in the interests of science – umpteen times.

Then he studied vile vomit. Amongst other disgusting discoveries he found that stomach acid could dissolve soft bone and gristle but this took longer than ordinary meat.

Disgusting digestion expressions
One doctor says to another:

I MAY BE ABOUT TO REGURGITATE

Should you take cover?

Answer: YES. It's the posh word for being sick.

This can be triggered by:
a) Fear – e.g. a science test.
b) A horrible sight or smell – e.g. a revolting science experiment.
c) Disgusting food or poison or germs – e.g. a school dinner.
Oddly enough, doctors also use the term to describe leaking of the blood from a dodgy valve in the heart.

A sickening story

You're dizzy, you turn pale, you sweat and your mouth is full of spit. You're about to chuck up. Run for the bathroom! The muscles in your lower body and stomach all squeeze together until your half-digested food erupts from your gullet. Vomiting, as it's called, is controlled by a part of your brain known as the vomiting centre. It's well-known that throwing up can be triggered by fear. Scientists don't quite know how this happens. They think that your nerves produce chemicals that make your stomach heave when you're scared of something.

What your vomit looks like depends on how long it's been in your stomach. If it's only been there for a few seconds it won't look too different from when you ate it. Especially if it happens to be carrot stew. But if it's been down for a couple of hours it will be a thick soupy mess. Scientists call this disgusting substance chyme (pronounced chime). How chyming, er, sorry, charming.

Could you be a scientist?

Have you ever bent over and thought you were about to be sick? Don't try to do it now – take my word for it, it happens. The half-digested food slips out of your stomach. The acid mixture can burn the oesophagus so

badly that some sufferers think they're having a heart attack. This is called heartburn. Some scientists looked at the effects of exercise on heartburn. They measured the amount of acid stomach juice there was in the oesophagus one hour after…
a) Running
b) Weightlifting
c) Cycling
Which do you think caused the most heartburn?

Unbearable ulcers

Life can be tough for the stomach, too. One of the nastiest things that can happen to a stomach is when it starts digesting itself! This is what's known as an ulcer. Ulcers can be unbearably painful and need to be treated with substances such as chalk (yes, chalk) that neutralize the acid.

Your stomach has three lines of defence.
1 A thick layer of jelly-like mucus (the same stuff as slimy, runny snot, remember). This stops the acid leaking out and causing an ulcer.
2 A wall of 800 million cells wedged together to block

any acid that does escape. The cells are being replaced and every three days you get a brand new shiny pink stomach lining!

3 If the stomach gets too acidic the cells make a chemical called bicarbonate of soda. This is actually the same chemical you find in alka-seltzer and other medicines that settle an upset tum. The chemical neutralizes the acid so it isn't so strong.

Normally, though, ulcers only happen to stressed-out grown-ups.

HOW ARE YOU GETTING ON WITH YEAR 5, MR SIMPKINS?

Scientists reckon that ulcers are caused by bacteria that stop the stomach lining from making so much lovely protective mucus. This allows the stomach's acid to make a hole in the lining – and that's the ulcer. Sounds painful.

Talking about the guts, which we were a moment ago, it's time to leave the stomach and check out the intestines. And the going is going to get seriously disgusting from now on.

POO-EY PONG

Welcome to the intestines – the most horrible bit of your digestive system. The place where it's all happening. It's where fats, carbohydrates and proteins get broken down to smaller chemicals and sucked into the blood. And it's home to all sorts of disgusting goings-on.

Remember Gutzache's epic journey through the guts? Here's the map he used. It'll help you find your way around this chapter, too.

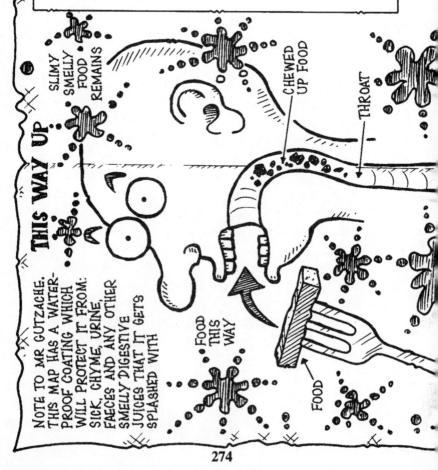

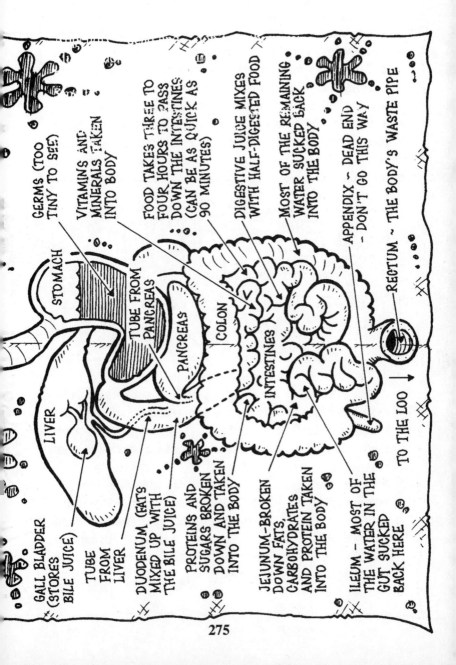

GERMS (TOO TINY TO SEE)

VITAMINS AND MINERALS TAKEN INTO BODY

FOOD TAKES THREE TO FOUR HOURS TO PASS DOWN THE INTESTINES (CAN BE AS QUICK AS 90 MINUTES)

DIGESTIVE JUICE MIXES WITH HALF-DIGESTED FOOD

MOST OF THE REMAINING WATER SUCKED BACK INTO THE BODY

APPENDIX ~ DEAD END ~ DON'T GO THIS WAY

RECTUM ~ THE BODY'S WASTE PIPE

STOMACH

TUBE FROM PANCREAS

PANCREAS

COLON

INTESTINES

LIVER

GALL BLADDER (STORES BILE JUICE)

TUBE FROM LIVER

DUODENUM (FATS MIXED UP WITH THE BILE JUICE)

PROTEINS AND SUGARS BROKEN DOWN AND TAKEN INTO THE BODY

JEJUNUM-BROKEN DOWN FATS, CARBOHYDRATES AND PROTEIN TAKEN INTO THE BODY

ILEUM - MOST OF THE WATER IN THE GUT SUCKED BACK HERE

TO THE LOO

275

Gruesome guts facts

1 The human intestines are nine metres (27 feet) long and if they weren't tightly coiled and curled up you'd have to be 11 metres (36 feet) tall to fit them all in.

2 The duodenum got its name after Greek doctor Herophilus (4th century BC) claimed it was 12 fingers long. ("Duodenum" means "12 fingers" in Greek.)

3 The ancient Greeks and Romans believed you could foretell the future by sacrificing a sheep to the gods and peering at its intestines. On the whole, the more unhealthy the intestines looked, the more unhealthy your future was supposed to be.

YOUR FUTURE LOOKS LITTLE BETTER THAN THE SHEEP'S

4 The inside of the small intestine looks like a furry carpet. The "fur" is thousands of tiny sticking out bits called villi that suck in digested food and transfer it to the blood. Ironed flat this area would cover 20-40 square metres (215-430 square feet) – about the size of a large classroom.

5 Gruesome stones made from waste food and minerals sometimes form in the guts. These bezoar (be-zo-ar) stones are also found in sheep and goat stomachs and were thought to have magical powers. In the 17th century they were ground up and used as medicines but they were as useless as a square football.

6 In fifth-century India doctors were not afraid to perform operations to remove blockages in the guts. They cut open the patient and afterwards joined the sides of the cut using … ants. Yes, ants. They got a giant black ant to bite the sides of the wound then cut the ant's head off. This left the jaws in position just like a little stitch. Luckily your guts can't feel pain apart from a bit of cramp. So at least the operation didn't hurt the human patient, even if the ants were a bit cut up about it.

Dare you discover … what bile juice does to fats?

What you need
washing-up liquid
a bowl of warm water
cooking oil

All you do is
1 Pour a little cooking oil into the water. The oil will float on the water. This is like the fat in your intestines.
2 Add a drop of the washing-up liquid representing the bile juice. Give the mixture a rapid stir.
What happens next?
a) The oil sinks to the bottom of the bowl and forms a kind of sludge.
b) The oil, washing-up liquid and water mix together in lots of little bubbles.

c) The oil, washing-up liquid and water form huge bubbles that don't burst easily.

Gruesome greetings

You might wonder how all this activity is controlled by your body. Why doesn't the food in one part of the intestine simply stop moving so that the rest of your supper piles up behind it?

In fact, special chemicals in the blood called hormones carry messages from one part of the body to another to control this vital job. Just imagine if you could hear these messages – what would they say?

One hormone is called secretin (see-creet-in) and here's its message...

Another hormone is called cholecystokinin (kole-sis-toe-ki-nin) – we'll let it speak for itself.

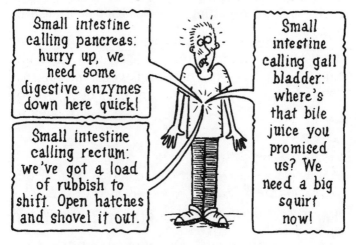

Small intestine calling pancreas: hurry up, we need some digestive enzymes down here quick!

Small intestine calling rectum: we've got a load of rubbish to shift. Open hatches and shovel it out.

Small intestine calling gall bladder: where's that bile juice you promised us? We need a big squirt now!

Meanwhile, the guts also keep in touch using nerves like a kind of telephone line. Let's listen in to a few more conversations

Small intestine to brain control centre: everything's under control. Things are moving nicely. No, hold on – looks like we've got a problem. It's an alien substance – could be a school dinner. Tell the vomiting centre it's action stations. Get ready to heave!

The grumbling appendix

Sometimes when the appendix gets infected by germs it swells up like a disgusting pus-filled balloon. It can even explode.

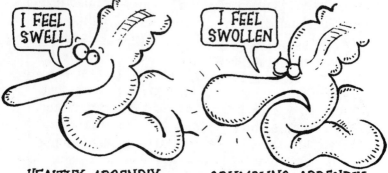

HEALTHY APPENDIX   GRUMBLING APPENDIX

This appalling ailment is called appendicitis and in serious cases the appendix has to be removed. But if the infection isn't too bad the body's white cells guzzle most of the germs and the appendix gets better. If the germs multiply again you get more pain. This delightful condition is known as a "grumbling appendix". No doubt it makes the patients grumble too. But it could be worse. It could be a dodgy colon.

Cut out the colon

The colon is 1.5 metres (5 feet) long. It's the last bit of the intestines and the name given to the : sign in punctuation. So don't be surprised if your teacher finds a "colon" in a library book. The colon stores your poo before it's pushed out of your body. During this time the walls of the colon suck much of the remaining water from the poo. This stops you spending your life on the toilet getting rid of watery diarrhoea.

Top surgeon Sir William Arbuthnot Lane (1856-1943) was keen on ballroom dancing and designing new types of surgical instruments. But he wasn't too keen on colons. He thought they were useless and caused disease when germs escaped from the colon to infect the body. And he claimed the victim smelt of graveyards. Willie also said people with dodgy colons had cold, bluish ears, cold noses, clammy sweaty hands and ...

Well, Willie was in the know when it came to colons. His claim to fame was to discover the sudden twists and turns in the colon now known as Lane's kinks.

Worried about the appearance of his patients, Willie invented an operation in which the offending colon was removed. This was fine, so long as the victim, sorry patient, didn't mind the consequences. These involved spending the rest of their life with a hole in their guts through which their poo passed into a bag. Yuk! Fortunately, other doctors criticised Lane for performing the operation unnecessarily. And so Lane's treatment of the colon came to a : er, sorry, a full stop.

Meanwhile, back in the intestines things are really hotting up. Boiling and bubbling as mysterious chemicals get to work. Enter the energetic enzymes. Is your gut getting fizz-ical? Better find out now...

Energetic enzymes

Look inside your body and you'll see a gruesome assembly of bones, muscles and blood. But look closer and you'll see a fizzing mass of chemical reactions that would make most chemists green with envy. It's all done with enzymes. Without them digestion would be a dead loss and so would you. But with them you're fizzing with physical fitness. So what do enzymes do all day?

Disgusting enzymes fact file

NAME: Enzymes

THE BASIC FACTS: **1** An enzyme is a protein that changes other chemicals. In digestion, enzymes break other chemicals to pieces.

2 Every cell in your body contains over 3,000 different enzymes.

THE HORRIBLE DETAILS: If you didn't have enzymes the only other way to digest your food would be to heat your body. This also breaks the food chemicals up. Unfortunately, your body would need to be 300°C (572°F) to do this. So you'd need to cook yourself to enjoy your food.

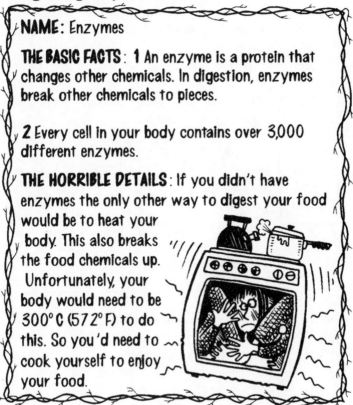

Dare you discover … how enzymes work?

What you need

a hard-boiled egg. (Ask an adult to help you boil the egg for ten minutes.) Cool the egg and peel off the shell.
biological washing powder
a jar
a spoon

All you do is

1 Add eight tablespoonfuls of warm water to the jar.

2 Mix in one tablespoonful of washing powder. Stir until the powder disappears.

3 Add a piece of the boiled egg white (not the yellow yolk).

4 Wrap the jar in a towel and leave in a warm place such as an airing cupboard for two days.

5 Take a look at the piece of egg white. What do you notice?

a) The egg is a horrible brown colour.

b) The egg has turned into a white liquid.

c) The egg has got smaller.

Bet you never knew!
Enzymes make heat as they rip chemicals to pieces
inside your guts. That's why Arctic sledge drivers give
their dogs butter to eat in very cold weather. Butter is
digested by enzymes and this makes enough heat to
warm the dogs. And if enzymes make heat, let's visit a
few hot spots.

Disgusting pancreas fact file

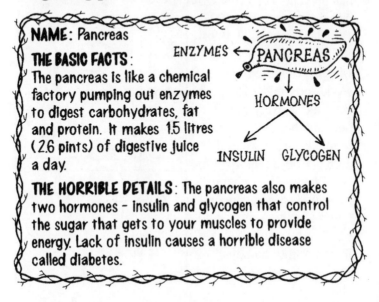

NAME: Pancreas

THE BASIC FACTS:
The pancreas is like a chemical
factory pumping out enzymes
to digest carbohydrates, fat
and protein. It makes 1.5 litres
(2.6 pints) of digestive juice
a day.

ENZYMES ← PANCREAS

HORMONES

INSULIN   GLYCOGEN

THE HORRIBLE DETAILS: The pancreas also makes
two hormones – insulin and glycogen that control
the sugar that gets to your muscles to provide
energy. Lack of insulin causes a horrible disease
called diabetes.

A worthy winner?

Scientists toil away for years until at last they make a great discovery. But who should get the glory for discoveries? Take insulin, for example. When scientists found out about insulin they were able to give extra insulin to people with diabetes. Thousands of lives were saved. In Sweden a committee met to award the 1923 Nobel Prize for Medicine... But who should get credit? These were the main contenders:

Frederick Banting (1891-1941)

A First World War hero. Like many scientists of his time, Banting was convinced there was something in the pancreas that prevented diabetes. He discovered insulin in 1922.

Charles Best (1899-1978)

Brilliant laboratory assistant who helped make Banting's work possible. He and Banting bravely injected one another with insulin to make sure it was safe.

James Collip (1892-1965)

A talented chemist. Showed Banting and Best how to make a pure kind of insulin suitable for injecting into humans.

John Macleod (1876-1935)
In charge of the lab in Canada where Banting and Best worked. Didn't think much of Banting as a scientist. Was on holiday when insulin was discovered.

Two scientists were awarded the coveted Nobel Prize in 1923 – but which two?

Disgusting liver fact file

NAME: Liver

THE BASIC FACTS: It's brown and weighs about 1.5kg (4.4lbs). It has hundreds of jobs including making bile which helps to digest fats. After food has been digested, the liver stores food chemicals and vitamins.

287

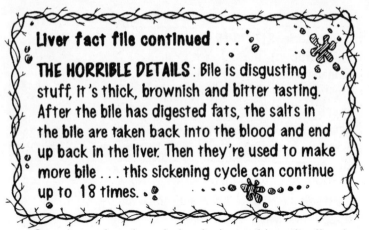

Liver fact file continued ...

THE HORRIBLE DETAILS: Bile is disgusting stuff, it's thick, brownish and bitter tasting. After the bile has digested fats, the salts in the bile are taken back into the blood and end up back in the liver. Then they're used to make more bile ... this sickening cycle can continue up to 18 times.

One man played a vital role in probing the liver's secrets...

Horrible Science Hall of Fame: Claude Bernard (1813-1878) Nationality: French

Bernard was the son of a humble grape picker but when he died he was the first French scientist to enjoy a full state funeral. Well, maybe "enjoy" isn't the right word since he was dead at the time. Young Claude Bernard didn't want to be a scientist. He wanted to be a playwright. Fortunately (for science), his plays were so bad that Claude took up medicine instead.

He discovered that carbohydrates are broken down into sugars during digestion and fats are broken down by bile juice. Then he found that the liver can make sugar. He fed a dog on a sugar-free diet and then opened up its liver to find that sugar had mysteriously appeared there.

Mrs Bernard was just one of many who believed that Claude's experiments were cruel to dogs. No dog owner would allow Claude near their pets and the scientist soon found that his programme of research was in trouble owing to a shortage of subjects.

So he took to kidnapping dogs for his research. One day one of Bernard's stolen dogs escaped from the lab and ran home to its owner. Unfortunately, the owner happened to be the Chief of Police and he came round to ask the scientist some awkward questions...

What do you think happened next?

a) Claude Bernard was sentenced to three years' hard labour for cruelty to dogs. Mrs Bernard was the chief prosecution witness.

b) The scientist was let off after paying a hefty fine and making a big donation to the local stray dogs home.

c) Bernard made a grovelling apology and was let off with a caution.

Answer

c) And you'll be pleased to know the dog lived happily ever after with his owner.

Disgusting liver diseases

The ancient peoples of Babylonia (modern Iraq) had a disgusting method of finding out what liver disease a person was suffering from. Let's take a look at this ancient tablet. *

* That's a clay tablet, not the sort of tablet you'd take for an upset tum or sore throat.

AN ANCIENT TABLET →

How to spot liver disease

You need one sheep

1. Blow into the sheep's nostrils
2. Sacrifice the sheep to the gods and look at its liver
3. Compare the liver to a clay model. If there's anything different about the real animal liver you'll have this problem, too.

AN ANCIENT TABLET ↘

Stones similar to those in the guts can also appear in the liver. They often form in the gall bladder where they do no harm unless they get big enough to stop bile from reaching the guts. If there is a blockage, the bile leaks into the blood and ends up in the skin and eyeballs. Bile contains colours made from waste chemicals from the liver and these turn the skin and eyeballs a tasteful yellow. This disgusting condition is known as jaundice.

CAN YOU TELL WHICH OF THESE YELLOW OBJECTS HAS JAUNDICE?

Nowadays, it's easy for surgeons to crush the stones or in the worst cases simply whip out the gall bladder in one easy operation. Meanwhile, your body is busy using up all your hard-digested food.

Juicy joules

Your blood carries the juicy digested food chemicals to all parts of your body. In your muscles the chemicals are ripped apart to produce the energy that keeps you going. We measure this energy in kilojoules (ke-lo-jools) or kJ for short.

Bet you never knew!
A boy aged 9-11 needs 9,500 kJ of food per day to keep going and between the ages of 12 and 14 this goes up to 11,000 kJ. A girl of 9-11 needs only 8,500 kJ per day and at 12-14 she needs 9,000 kJ. So why do girls need less food? Some girls are smaller or less active than boys. Or maybe they're just not so greedy.

Compare that with...
• A canary needs just 46 kJ a day to avoid hopping off its perch for good.
• An elephant uses up a jumbo 385,000 kJ a day.
• A rocket needs 100,000,000 (one hundred million) kJ to get into space.
Confusing isn't it? Maybe this quiz will help you digest the facts.

Energy quiz

Can you find the food with the right amount of energy to keep you going through each challenge?

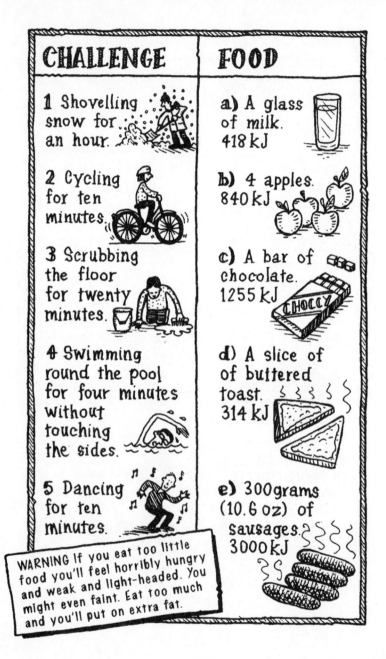

CHALLENGE	FOOD
1 Shovelling snow for an hour.	**a)** A glass of milk. 418 kJ
2 Cycling for ten minutes.	**b)** 4 apples. 840 kJ
3 Scrubbing the floor for twenty minutes.	**c)** A bar of chocolate. 1255 kJ
4 Swimming round the pool for four minutes without touching the sides.	**d)** A slice of of buttered toast. 314 kJ
5 Dancing for ten minutes.	**e)** 300 grams (10.6 oz) of sausages. 3000 kJ

WARNING If you eat too little food you'll feel horribly hungry and weak and light-headed. You might even faint. Eat too much and you'll put on extra fat.

A hot problem

Producing all that energy also generates heat. That's why you feel really hot and sweaty after a run. Every day we produce the same heat as burning 500g (1 lb) of coal. Twelve people sitting in a room give off as much heat as a small electric fire. Luckily, the blood takes the heat outwards to the skin where it escapes into the air through the pores in your skin. Phew – that's a relief!

Sometimes the heat takes water away from your body in the form of sweat and this also cools you down. But if you've got too much water in your body there's another way to get rid of it. Any idea what that might be?

FLUSH

Going round the bend

You can't get away from the toilet. Ultimately it will command your presence with all the power of a giant magnet. Once your breakfast has worked its way through your system, your body will insist on it. It doesn't matter how busy you are – even if it's the middle of a vital science test. You've gotta do what you've gotta do.

But why? The story starts with a couple of rather crucial organs – the kidneys.

Crucial kidneys fact file

NAME: Kidneys

THE BASIC FACTS: You've got two – one on either side of your body – although you only need one to stay alive. Each one is about 11 x 6cm (4 x 2 inches) and its job is to filter spare water and waste chemicals from your blood.

THE HORRIBLE DETAILS: The waste stuff is urine – that's pee to you.

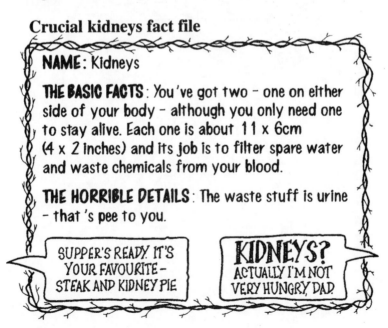

Fantastic filters

Every day about 2,000 litres (440 gallons) of blood flows through your kidneys. Now, as you may have noticed, you don't have that much blood. So we're talking about the same blood going through the kidneys lots of times.

Here's what happens…

Just imagine your kidneys as a pair of fantastic coffee filters. (They do filter coffee along with everything else.)

LEFT KIDNEY

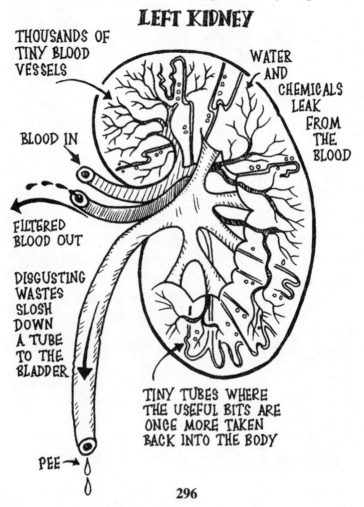

THOUSANDS OF TINY BLOOD VESSELS

WATER AND CHEMICALS LEAK FROM THE BLOOD

BLOOD IN

FILTERED BLOOD OUT

DISGUSTING WASTES SLOSH DOWN A TUBE TO THE BLADDER

TINY TUBES WHERE THE USEFUL BITS ARE ONCE MORE TAKEN BACK INTO THE BODY

PEE →

THIS KIDNEY MACHINE FROM 50 YEARS AGO COULD KEEP A PATIENT ALIVE WHILE A DAMAGED KIDNEY HEALED

Disgusting digestion expressions

COFFEE?

BETTER NOT, I MIGHT HAVE MICTURITION (MICK-TUR-RISH-EON) PROBLEMS

Shouldn't she be in hospital?

Useless urine facts

Shock the whole school with the extent of your useless knowledge.

1 Most adults produce 1-2 litres (0.2-0.4 gallons) of urine a day. That's 40,000 litres (8,000 gallons) in a lifetime, enough to fill 500 baths. (Warning: it's extremely anti-social to pee in one bath, let alone 500.)

2 By the time the bladder has about 0.3 litres (0.07 gallons) it's already feeling full and needs to take a leak.

3 When the bladder fills up, its sides stretch until they're as thin as an onion skin.

4 The opening at the bottom of the bladder is operated by the brain. That's why you don't wet yourself (or at least not very often). Babies don't know how to do this and that's why they wear nappies. When you go to sleep, messages from your brain keep the opening locked to prevent little disasters in the night.

5 When you go to the toilet you usually hold your breath. (It's true – see what happens next time you pee.) This allows the diaphragm, a muscle above your liver, to push down on your guts. This in turn squashes the bladder and forces the urine to squirt down its exit tube.

6 Urine is about 96 per cent water. The rest is a mix of urea (remember, that's a waste chemical made by your body), and a bit of waste protein and salt. It's a bit smelly but it's usually germ-free…

7 That's why urine was once used to wash wounds on the battlefield. No need to try this next time you get a cut.

GO ON THEN, IF YOU REALLY THINK IT WILL HELP

8 Most of the time urine is yellow – that's the urea. But sometimes it can be a different colour – such as red, that's when you've eaten too much beetroot. And disgusting facts such as this were once incredibly useful to a breed of...

Useless urine doctors

Sometimes your doctor will ask for a sample of your urine. This can help to detect certain diseases. But for hundreds of years doctors thought that you could identify every kind of disease by looking at the patient's urine. Some doctors even tasted it, too. Erk!

In the Middle Ages Spanish urine doctor, Arnold of Villanova, said:

If you find nothing wrong with the patient's urine, but he still insists he has a headache, tell him it is an obstruction of the liver. Continue to speak of obstruction, it is a word he won't understand, but it sounds important.

Surely doctors aren't like that nowadays. They wouldn't use long words just to confuse their patients ... would they?

Disgusting expressions

ARE YOU HAVING PROBLEMS WITH YOUR DEFAECATION?

How should she answer? Clue: it's nothing to do with Christmas paper chains, they're *decorations*.

Answer Defaecation is the posh medical term for making poo. For most people this is once a day or once every two days. But people who eat lots of fibre can defaecate *five times* per day. Bet they get through a fortune in loo rolls.

Foul faeces

You remember all that waste food piling up in the colon? Well, it's got to go some time. So every day some of it is shoved out of the anus – usually about 150g (22 oz) for a child. About three-quarters of this is water and the rest is waste food such as fibre and dead germs. Lovely!

Note: anus = the hole in your bum where the waste products come out. Not to be confused with Uranus which is a distant planet. Clearly you wouldn't want your anus to be that distant.

Could you be a scientist?

You are a doctor. Two patients see you. One says ...
Doctor, doctor, my poo is red.

1 What do you say?

a) It's blood. You'll be dead in a week.

b) You've got a liver disease that's turned your bile red.

c) Stop eating so many tomatoes.

The other patient says...

Doctor, doctor, my poo is blue!

2 What do you say?

a) You have a rare colon disease.

b) That's impossible – you must be an alien.

c) Stop eating those blackberries.

Crunched-up constipation

When you're very worried you'd think your body would help you feel better. But it doesn't. Instead the vagus nerve for some reason doesn't send the signals from the brain that make you go to the toilet. As a result the poo piles up in the colon where its moisture is sucked back into the blood. The poo becomes dry and crammed together – that's constipation. So it's painful to get rid of – and that really is a worry. And here's another worry – sometimes stress can speed up peristalsis resulting in diarrhoea and extra farts.

If this happens to you, maybe you'd like to try Sir William Arbuthnot Lane's patent constipation remedy...

COD LIVER OIL (MADE FROM DEAD FISH)

OLIVE OIL

CONSTIPATION CURE

LIQUID PARAFFIN (IDEAL FUEL FOR LAMPS)

JUST ONE TEASPOON WILL KEEP YOU GOING ALL DAY!

The paraffin acts like oil in a rusty bike chain. It gets the poo moving again. No, on second thoughts better not – you wouldn't want your guts to turn into a paraffin lamp would you now? And there are enough dangerous gases down there already.

Disgusting digestion expressions

YOU'VE GOT A FLATULENCE PROBLEM

Does this need surgery?

Answer:
No, just a clothes peg over the nose. Flatulence is the scientific name for farting. It's nothing to do with being flat – although you might feel a bit flattened after being given this diagnosis.

Ten things you always wanted to know about farting but were afraid to ask

1 Kings and Queens fart. Presidents fart and so do Emperors. Children fart and even teachers are said to do it once in a while. The only difference is how much, how often and how loudly they let it out.

2 The first known account of farting was by ancient Greek playwright Aristophanes (about 448-380 BC) who makes a character in one of his plays say,

"My wind exploded like a thunderclap."

Sounds nasty.

3 Farting is simply your body's way of getting rid of air that you've swallowed by eating too fast, talking while eating, or swallowing bubbly spit. Of course, you can burp some air up. The more you burp, the less you fart. Better not try explaining this important principle at family meal-times.

IT'S YOUR FAULT MUM – YOU DON'T LIKE ME BURPING!

WHIFF

FARTY SMELL

PONG

Or this one…

4 This air gets mixed up with poo in the gut. If there's a lot of air in poo it'll float.

5 Amazingly, a group of fearless scientists analysed the chemical ingredients of a fart. (Did they wear gas masks?) They bravely discovered that a fart is a mixture of five different gases – mainly nitrogen (59 per cent) which is a boring gas that floats about in the air without people taking too much notice of it. Except when someone farts!

6 Well, the smell comes from the chemicals indole and skatole. These are given off when germs get to work on bits of protein from your food.

7 Sometimes a gas called hydrogen sulphide forms in farts. This happens when chemicals from different foods get together in the guts. You'll know all about it because the fart smells like rotten eggs. It's bad news – and not only in the social sense. Hydrogen sulphide is poisonous and it can explode if too much of it mixes with oxygen in the air.

Crisps are full of little air bubbles. Chewing gum makes you swallow air. Like the air in crisps this may re-emerge as farts. Fizzy drinks are full of bubbles.

8 Beans, brussel sprouts, cauliflowers and bran contain a type of carbohydrate that the germs in your gut can change into gas.

Scientists reckon that meat contains many of the chemicals that cause some of the smelliest farts.

9 US astronauts are banned from eating certain foods, especially beans, before a space-flight. Well, how would you fancy being cooped up in a cramped spacecraft on a ten-day space mission with someone who had a bit of a bottom problem?

10 Mind you, flying can make you fart. As a plane flies higher the air pressure around the passengers drops. This makes the air in the guts expand and the result is . . . well, I think you can guess.

When it comes to getting rid of smells there is one invention that has proved more than a flush in the pan.

Flushed with success

1 The first loo that could be flushed with water was in the palace of Knossos, Crete. This 3,500-year-old loo even had a bung you could stick down the pan to block nasty whiffs from the sewers.

2 In the Middle Ages most people had toilets that were nothing more than seats over smelly holes in the ground.

3 In 1590, Englishman Sir John Harrington invented a loo that could be flushed with water.

4 But the loo really came into its own after 1778 when inventor Joseph Bramah devised the ball valve which automatically filled the cistern and the "U" bend.

5 Gradually toilets became more and more popular with anyone rich enough to afford them.

But there was a problem.

Something in the air

The problem had been festering for some time, growing ever more gross, ever nastier with each passing year. And with each year the truth became ever more unpalatable, ever more horrible. London, one of the greatest cities in the world, stank. It didn't just pong, whiff or smell – it STANK. By the 1850s it reeked of rotting sewage and filth and every kind of loathsome rubbish. And it stank because London's sewerage system had broken down.

The London Times

4th August 1857

A BIG JOB?

Today we bring you an exclusive interview with genuine London "tosher" - Bert Smellie.

Bert's unenviable job is to crawl into the sewers in search of valuables accidentally flushed down toilets.

On a good day Bert finds coins, bits of rag and bones. "The work's all right," he says, "it's good money but it's dangerous too!"

"What sort of dangers?" I ask him.

"Them sewers is diabolical," says Bert. "Falling to bits - they can fall on you without warning and you'd be

Bert Smellie

buried alive. Others have deep pools that'll suck you down in rotten slime. And the smell is bad enough to make you heave.

"And then there's the rats. Yeah. Giant rats big as cats some of them. At night they come out of the sewers into houses. They've been known to attack babies. Even some of my mates have been attacked by rats. All we ever found was their skeletons. Horrible . . . and to think, it could have been me."

"Come off it Bert," I laugh. "Pull the other one!"

Then Bert holds up one of his hands. It's covered in white scars. Rat bites.
Blimey!

The Editor writes . . .

We at the *London Times* say something must be done about this disgrace. London must have new sewers. The politicians must get their act together and pay for it . . . this issue STINKS and we believe there's a real whiff of corruption here.

Eventually the sewers couldn't take it any more. And so began the Great Stink. It was the most horrible smell anyone could remember. In the hot summer of 1858 the smell of the sewage-clogged River Thames was so foul that people were physically sick. Eventually people kicked up such a stink about it that the politicians were forced to act. The problem was so urgent that the Government agreed to fork out for a brand new sewerage system. At once!

Super sewers

In all, 209 km (130 miles) of new sewers were constructed. They mainly ran downhill to take the waste away from London. And the system is still operating today. Nowadays complex sewage systems are commonplace in large cities. But in the 19th century some of them were considered so amazing that they became tourist attractions. Can you imagine it?

For a holiday with a difference . . .

The Municipal Sewage Experience

GREAT VALUE - IT WON'T BE A DRAIN ON YOUR POCKET!

A unique thrilling close-up view of how our fascinating sewage system deals with waste water from washing and toilets, and rainwater from gutters.

GASP WITH AMAZEMENT

as the watery mass of sewage is filtered to remove large objects and then left to settle.

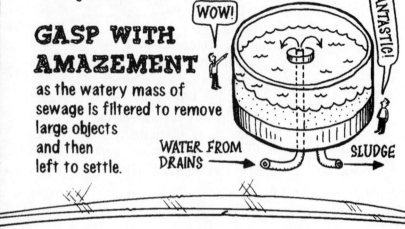

WOW!

FANTASTIC!

WATER FROM DRAINS →

SLUDGE

BE TOTALLY GOBSMACKED

as watery waste is left in tanks where much of it is eaten by hungry germs. Or we can use the poison chlorine to bump them off!

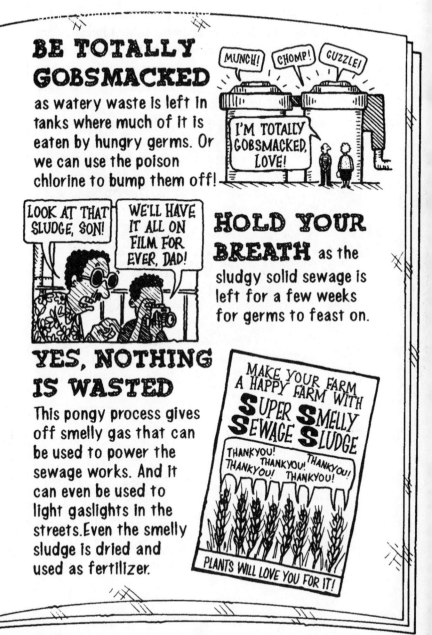

MUNCH! CHOMP! GUZZLE!

I'M TOTALLY GOBSMACKED, LOVE!

LOOK AT THAT SLUDGE, SON!

WE'LL HAVE IT ALL ON FILM FOR EVER, DAD!

HOLD YOUR BREATH as the

sludgy solid sewage is left for a few weeks for germs to feast on.

YES, NOTHING IS WASTED

This pongy process gives off smelly gas that can be used to power the sewage works. And it can even be used to light gaslights in the streets. Even the smelly sludge is dried and used as fertilizer.

MAKE YOUR FARM A HAPPY FARM WITH SUPER SMELLY SEWAGE SLUDGE

THANKYOU! THANKYOU! THANKYOU! THANKYOU! THANKYOU!

PLANTS WILL LOVE YOU FOR IT!

So sewage makes excellent plant food! Ideally suited for growing crops. Crops to make into a school lunch.

A school lunch. But that's where this book started, isn't it?

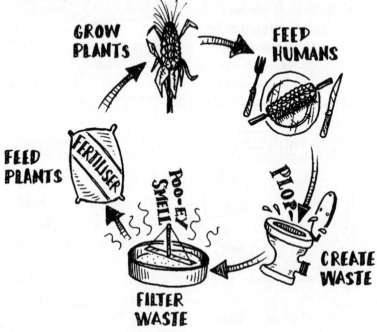

GROW PLANTS

FEED HUMANS

FEED PLANTS

FERTILISER

POO-EY SMELL

PLOP

CREATE WASTE

FILTER WASTE

Something to chew over
(food for thought)

Food's brilliant. We think about it, we talk about it, we even dream about it. And when it's on our plates we play with it before we eat it. But what goes inside our bodies is even more fascinating.

If your digestive system was a machine it would be the most amazing and incredible machine ever invented. Every day it systematically sorts through whatever you choose to feed it with. It sorts out the bits your body can use and chucks out the bits it can't.

All the time you're busy watching TV, sitting in a science lesson or chatting with your friends, your guts are quietly (leaving aside the odd gurgle) getting on with this vital task. They hardly ever protest – OK, so they make you throw up from time to time, but only if they've got a good reason.

So how long has it taken you to read the first bit of this chapter? About one minute? Right, prepare to be amazed... In just one minute:

• Your stomach has churned three times.

• 500,000 new cells have been made for lining your stomach.

• The food in your guts has moved 2.5cm (1 inch).

• And your kidneys might have filtered out 1.4ml (0.05 fl oz) of urine that even now could be trickling into your bladder.

• Meanwhile all the glands and organs in your digestive system are happily pumping and squirting away: salivary glands, stomach, liver pancreas. All of them producing their vital juices and enzymes.

And so it carries on 24 hours a day. Even when you're asleep. Even when you're in a Science lesson and not thinking about food at all. You've got to admit, it's fascinatingly disgusting.

312

HORRIBLE SCIENCE

Science with the squishy bits left in!

Also available:

Ugly Bugs
The insect world goes under the magnifying glass.
Observe some foul families of bugs, discover the
secrets of strange scientists and test the theories of
insect disguise. It's swarming with info!

Blood, Bones and Body Bits
This book will get right under your skin! Test the theories
of your own brain power, discover the secrets of strange
scientists and learn how to diagnose deadly diseases.

Nasty Nature
Have a whale of a time finding out about the animal
world! Grapple with some very ferocious creatures,
meet some nosey naturalists and learn how to get on
with a gorilla. You'll be howling for more!

Chemical Chaos
Put chaotic chemistry to the test! Uncover the facts
about experiments that went horribly wrong, discover
the secrets of strange scientists and try your hand at
quirky chemistry in your own kitchen.

Fatal Forces
Can you resist the urge to discover why your ears stop
you falling off your bike? You'll also find out what
keeps the moon in the sky, how quickly your fingernails
grow ... and what happens when an apple smacks a
scientist on the bonce!

Sounds Dreadful
Lift the lid on noise and find out how sound waves make
your ear drums tremble, how a microphone turns your
voice into electrical pulses ... and why you might get a
nose bleed listening to church bells. It's a real scream!

Evolve or Die
Why are we still here when other creatures have been
turned to stone, for ever? Go back millions of years to
see insects as big as birds, fish with teeth and why
chimps could be related to you.

Vicious Veg
Get stuck into a feast of info. and discover which plants
eat dead insects for breakfast, why stinging nettles grow
on old skeletons and which fungi can make your toes
drop off. It's bloomin' amazing!

Frightening Light
Discover what stops your eyeballs from falling out,
why dead bodies can make ghostly glowing lights and
how a laser beam can sizzle human flesh. It's blazing
with info!

Suffering Scientists Special
Read the painful potted history of scientists and their
discoveries, from the first Greek brainboxes to modern-
day geniuses.

Deadly Diseases
From the common cold to shocking smallpox, find out what happens when your body comes under attack from germs. You'll meet some seriously dangerous diseases.

Look out for:

The Awfully Big Quiz Book
Do you have what it takes to challenge a chemist or fool a physicist? The Awfully Big Quiz Book is packed with hundreds of astounding science questions for testing your friends, your teachers ... and yourself.

Microscopic Monsters
Find out how toilet germs helped catch a thief, which creature lays eggs between your toes, why your toothbrush is covered in germs and what makes your guts the perfect home for bacteria. This is the tiny world of Science!

Explosive Experiments Special
A collection of experiments that will blow your mind! Find out how famous scientists made some of their most important discoveries and how you can test a few theories at home!

Science has never been so horrible!

Horrible Geography

Geography with the gritty bits left in!

Have you seen:

Odious Oceans

Read our roving reporter's guide to the seabed, uncover the dreadful details of the Titanic's last day and see if you're nautical enough to join the Navy.

Violent Volcanoes

Find out about volcano survivors, and get clued-up with the spotter's guide to eruptions.

Raging Rivers

Join our heroic hydrologists on a turbulent river tour from ice cap to ocean, read the secret diary of a brave river explorer and find out about watery wildlife.

Desperate Deserts

Visit the desert where it snows, find out how to make a tasty pudding from camel milk and why cactus juice could be a deadly drink.

Look out for:

Earth-shattering Earthquakes

See what it takes to make the earth shake, and what you should do if you're caught in an earthquake.

Freaky Peaks

Follow the adventures of mountain explorers, see the animals that live there, the plants that survive up mountains ... and whether or not the yeti really exists.